COMMONSENSE LOYALTY MARKETING

The Loyalty Journey......
From Intention to Action

Mala Raj, CLMP™

qurate
quratebooks.com

COMMONSENSE LOYALTY MARKETING
The Loyalty Journey from Intention to Action
Mala Raj, CLMP™

© Mala Raj, CLMP™

Published in 2024

© **Published by**

Qurate Books Pvt. Ltd.
Goa 403523, India
www.quratebooks.com
Tel: 1800-210-6527, Email: info@quratebooks.com

ISBN: 978-81-19263-91-2

ACKNOWLEDGEMENTS

Cliched but true! This book would have never even seen the light of day if it had not been for the constant prodding, pushing, encouragement, and yes, even nagging – from my husband Raj Raman - to get me to actually put fingers to keyboard and document my years of loyalty experience. Thank you for the unshakeable belief and faith shown. You have truly been the wind beneath my wings.

I owe a deep debt of gratitude to COLLOQUY™ (the erstwhile powerhouse repository of knowledge in Loyalty) and the Loyalty Academy, USA – my immense learning from both these sources, tempered by years of my own experience, has influenced the contents of this book.

This is the time to thank all those who contributed to my valuable years in CRM, Direct Marketing and Loyalty – R. Sridhar at OgilvyOne, Leena Basrur at Direxions, Sandeep Mittal at Cartesian and Anurag Saxena at Collinson. I would like to especially call out Brian Almeida with whom I worked the longest in Loyalty – at Direxions and later at Strategic Caravan. Thank you Brian. Working with you has been my most valuable stint in Loyalty.

Extremely special thanks are due to Bill Hanifin, CEO Wise Marketer Group, a globally known and respected expert in the field himself – for painstakingly going through the manuscript and agreeing to write the foreword. Very humbled and honoured by his contribution. Thank you, Bill. Look forward to sharing the mic with you again at Loyalty Academy™ workshops!

Thanks to all the teams who worked with me across clients and agencies and added to my learning and knowledge.

And, finally, the two other people at home who rejoice at every achievement in true happiness and are ever ready to celebrate with us – my son Abhishek and my daughter-in-law Roshnee. Thank you for being there.

FOREWORD

BILL HANIFIN, CLMP™

CEO, WISE MARKETER GROUP

In one of the first segmentation exercises that I participated in with a client, someone on our team came up with a cohort labelled as the "promiscuous customer". The use of this term took some people in the room by surprise. How dare we use a term with overtones that might offend the client?

As this happened nearly 20 years ago, the reaction should have been predictable. The team quickly highlighted the secondary definition for this word in the dictionary - "demonstrating an undiscriminating or unselective approach to a situation", in order to make its point clear. The message was that customers are fickle. Their attention is hard to command for any extended period of time and, just when you think the numbers are in your favour, they are easily swayed to another brand, offer, or campaign.

It's no wonder that the long game of customer loyalty has continually been challenged by the sugary sweet temptation of discounts and price wars. The unpredictable shopping behaviour demonstrated by consumers has been accentuated as we continue to emerge from a global pandemic and find our way into a life that we can describe as a new normal, but in reality, it is simply "new."

It is within this context that I was delighted to read **Commonsense Loyalty Marketing**, this new book written by Mala Raj, one of a handful of people that is qualified to document the essential knowledge of Loyalty Marketing. I have known Mala since my days working with the Colloquy Consulting Group and have watched her career flourish as she turned wise strategy into successful customer loyalty programs for the likes of BPCL, Levi's, Kaya, LuLu, Jockey, Titan, Ashok Leyland, bookmyshow, Cleartrip, Domino's and many more - in her work with Cartesian Consulting, Collinson, Strategic Caravan and others. In more recent times, I have shared the "mic" with Mala to deliver Loyalty Academy™ training.

The world is changing, and we need to embrace that change, applying innovative approaches to customer engagement and loyalty in response to modern technology, cultural norms, and preferences. I believe that as we look forward, we will find more success if we build on a solid foundation of knowledge. In this book, Mala shares her accumulated experience collaborating with clients, to map out the full complement of loyalty marketing essential principles and best practices.

Throughout the book, Mala channels the loyalty marketing mantra that "it's not that hard," a true statement in theory, but we see many programs in the market that suggest that the process of building effective loyalty programs is harder than we think. Read this book and you might find it "not that hard" to create more effective strategies and programs in your business.

This book is an easy read and could serve as a textbook in a university setting, something that is much needed. Wise Marketer Group created the Loyalty Academy to educate professionals in the business of customer-centricity and Commonsense Loyalty is ideal companion reading material to anyone seeking knowledge in this business. I recommend Commonsense Loyalty as a reference book that you can keep handy in your office and draw upon as you work to build value across your customer universe.

Contents

CHAPTER 1

IT'S NOT THAT HARD!

"Begin at the beginning," the King said, very gravely, "And go on till you come to the end: then stop." Alice In Wonderland

Welcome to the World of Loyalty!

There was a time a few years ago when, as a loyalty practitioner and trainer, I would ask people to open their wallets and count how many "Loyalty Cards" they had. The answers were revealing - not just to me – but also to themselves. The number of cards hidden in the recesses of slots in the wallet came as a surprise.

Today, the question is not entirely relevant. Cards are not a key identification instrument any more – we become members with mobile numbers – in some cases with mobile apps.

And therein lies the conundrum. We are all inextricably a part of this world of loyalty – more than we realise. All of us are members of various programs across categories – many of them we do not even recall.

The concept is familiar to all of us in the business of brands – yet, not quite clear! We think we know it – or should. And yet, do we actually?

When one says "Loyalty Marketing" what are the thoughts/terms that spring to mind?

"Points"

"Membership Card"

"Technology"

"Infrastructure"

"CRM?"

"Loyalty Program"

"Loyalty Engine"

Also - *"Takes ages to set up" "Huge investments" "When will it pay off for me?"*

Rolling eyes

Look of scepticism

So, let's start off on a comforting note. **It's really not that hard! And it's really common sense!**

And that's the purpose of this book. To take us through the journey of loyalty from start to finish – the rules, the ramifications, the decisions, the impact - and the inexorable joy of being a part of this world.

Every business wants customers to be loyal. Which means Loyalty Marketing really should be integral to every business plan. You acquire customers, you want them to stay with you. Acquiring new customers is **4-6 times as expensive** as retaining your existing ones! So it should be a no-brainer.

What this book attempts to do, is get down to first principles. We get to understand what constitutes loyalty, what are the different ways of building loyalty and how you go about designing for loyalty. We will cover the A to Z of loyalty design principles and practices. And readers will realise that what it really takes is diligence, eye for detail and a commitment to stay in the game. **It's not that hard!**

A QUICK OVERVIEW OF BASIC CONCEPTS – Or Loyalty 101 if you like!

What is Loyalty?

Loyalty is the "state of being true, steadfast in allegiance, faithful, dependable, unfailing, DEVOTED."

> *Late in the last century, a Russian nobleman lay on his deathbed.*
>
> *His anxious wife had one last question for him: 'Alexei, have you been faithful to me?'*
>
> *With his dying breath he turned to her and replied:*
>
> " Frequently"

What is CUSTOMER Loyalty?

Customer Loyalty is when customers of your brand remain true and devoted to your brand through thick and thin.

If we were to *define* loyalty, then we would perhaps say: **A deep commitment to rebuy a preferred product or service consistently in the future, in spite of situational influences and competitive marketing efforts that might cause switching.**

And what is LOYALTY MARKETING?

It is marketing differentially to your customer base to build their loyalty and repeat custom with you *for the long term.*

There are however some questions we need to ask ourselves:

1. Is a "frequent" or "consistent" customer LOYAL?

2. Is a loyal customer someone who gives you 100% of his/her business?

3. Can Loyalty be measured in market share?

4. Do you have to be a customer to be loyal to a brand?

And no, the answers are not that obvious!

Let's take each one:

1. **Is a "frequent" or "consistent" customer LOYAL?** Imagine a scenario where you live in a gated community with just one convenience store in the premises. You use that store for all your regular purchases. Every time you enter or leave your building you perhaps remember to pick something up from the store. You are consistent and regular. And frequent. But are you LOYAL? You seem to be so. But then imagine a scenario where a second store opens up just outside the gated community. Will you stick to the first store or will you

switch? That is the true test of your loyalty. So, in a nutshell – a "frequent" customer is not always a "loyal" customer

2. **Is a loyal customer someone who gives you 100% of his/her business?** I recall a time when Indian Airlines was the only domestic airline in the country. If you had to fly, you flew IA. 100% of your air travel spend was with IA. Were you loyal to IA? We know what happened when the skies opened up. Yes, there were some flyers who continued to fly IA. They were the loyalists. The rest switched, alternated, flirted with many. The same is true with Indian Railways today. Right now, every train journey we take in India is with Indian Railways, though privatisation is on the cards. Not so in the west. In the UK, there are 28 major train operators and you choose the one you want to use, much like airlines. 100% of your spend, does not necessarily mean loyalty.

3. **Can Loyalty be measured in market share?** Look around you for iPhone, iPod, Mac users. And hear them talk about their equipment. Can anyone question the "loyalty" that Apple users have for the brand? And yet, Apple was, till recently, not the market leader in phones or laptops in the US (Samsung and Dell close competitors respectively). And it is certainly not the market leader in India. What Apple has created is something like a "cult" of loyal users who will continue to use the brand and advocate it passionately. The same goes with Harley Davidson and the HOG (Harley Owners Group). As the cult grows, it will reflect in market share too, for sure. But market share is not always the indicator of loyalty to the brand.

4. **And, finally, do you have to be a "Customer" to be loyal to a brand?** Do you have a favourite football club or IPL team or music band? Or favourite car? Do you keep yourself updated on all the news and statistics about your sports clubs, all the features and gizmos of your favourite car? Who can question your passion or "loyalty" to Manchester United when you

watch them play on TV? But what have you actually SPENT on the brand? Have you bought tickets and watched them live? Have you spent money on merchandise at the stadium store? Have you bought a Ferrari? Or a Harley Davidson? Fandom is also loyalty - without related "purchase" behaviour.

What does this tell us? There is an EMOTIONAL component to LOYALTY that is as critical as the BEHAVIOURAL component. Emotional loyalty is when you FEEL strongly positive about the brand. Behavioural loyalty is when you demonstrate your loyalty in transactional behaviour with the brand. And there is scientific proof that there is a link between Emotional and Behavioural loyalty.

LOOKING AT YOUR CUSTOMER BASE THROUGH THE LOYALTY LENS

Let's see how you would look at your customer base using the filters of emotional and behavioural loyalty.

But first, typically, this is how you would segment your brand's customer base: In terms of current value and potential value

	Low Current Value High	
High Potential Value	Nurture and Grow	Invest and Protect
Low	Watch	Reinforce

Current Value is indicated by current transaction behaviour with the brand.

Potential value is indicated by trends in behaviour (growing trend) and use of surrogates (lifestyle variables, demographics) that would imply high potential to grow.

And how you would treat each segment would differ:

1. NURTURE AND GROW the segment which has low current value but displays high potential value. What will help bring this potential to reality?

2. INVEST IN AND PROTECT the segment where both Current and Potential value is high. You want them to retain current behaviour and you will continue to drive them to achieve their potential with you

3. REINFORCE current behaviour in the segment showing high current value but low potential to grow. You want to extend their lifecycle with you for as long as possible.

4. WATCH the segment that is low on both current and potential value. You never know when they start displaying characteristics of growth or potential.

ADDING THE EMOTIONAL AND BEHAVIOURAL LOYALTY DIMENSION

But here is how you would look at your base through the Loyalty lens:

	Low	Emotional	High
High	Prisoners		Happy Marriage
Low (Behavioural)	Strangers		Distant Lovers

These are the broad segments any customer base will fall into. Let's look at the four quadrants:

1. At the bottom left we have STRANGERS. They have low emotional and behavioural loyalty. They don't feel for the brand, they don't spend on the brand either. Minimal marketing investment would be allocated to this segment, if we could identify who they are.

2. At the bottom right we have DISTANT LOVERS. They feel very strongly for the brand but have shown low or nil transaction behaviour. Would we invest in them? Perhaps. If they have potential to grow the emotional loyalty for the brand by spreading the word - or have potential to grow their transaction behaviour.

3. At the top left we have PRISONERS. This is a dangerous and vulnerable segment. They transact regularly but have no emotional equity for the brand. The moment they get a viable

choice, they're going to move. Important to build a relationship beyond the transactional with this segment. Make them FEEL GOOD about choosing the brand. REASSURE them about their behaviour.

4. And at the top right is where every brand wants all their customers to be. HAPPY MARRIAGE. They feel strongly about your brand and transact regularly as well. This group is your MOST VALUABLE CUSTOMER group. The brand needs to protect, nurture, ring-fence this group.

Suddenly, your strategy gets a new dimension. It is not only about how your customers transact currently with the brand or how they're likely to in the future. It is also about how they FEEL towards your brand. And what you need to do to build that emotional equity which will ultimately translate into more business. Customers "feel" more today. They will transact more tomorrow. That's a fact.

THE LOYALTY LADDER

Next, let's look at where Loyalty fits into the marketing framework.

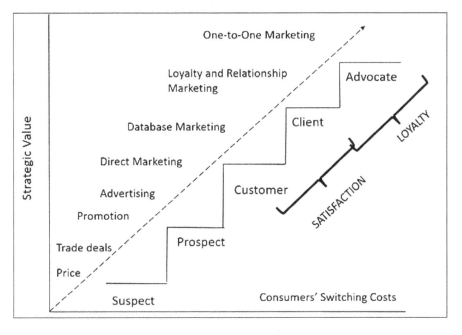

Let's understand the journey from Suspect to Advocate. You're launching a brand and you're building a marketing plan for it.

1. **Suspects** - The audience group you believe will be the target for this brand. You will broadly use product characteristics, price band, relevance etc to define this group

2. **Prospects** – Those amongst the audience group who have demonstrated some interest in your brand. They responded to your advertising. They attended an event. They called the customer care with queries. Advertising, promotions, trade offers – all these help build an interested prospect base.

3. **Customers** – Those who buy your brand for the first time. This may have been in response to your advertising – or to some direct targeting that you did to identifiable prospect groups. They are now your customers.

4. **Clients** – Once a customer is SATISFIED with his/her purchase, they repeat. They then become CLIENTS. This is where you use Database Marketing. You have a database of your customers and you use that to build a relationship with them.

5. **Advocates** – From Client to Advocate is really the **loyalty jump**. You want your clients to start advocating you. This means they have gone beyond satisfaction to a deeper commitment. Loyalty if you will. To enable this jump, the brand uses loyalty and relationship marketing programs. They may take many forms, which we will read about later in the book. And once an advocate, the brand builds a special one-to-one relationship with the customer. Such customers become ambassadors of the brand.

The goal of Loyalty Marketing is to move customers to the client and advocacy rungs. Loyalty Marketing does not play much of a role in customer acquisition – unlike what most marketers believe. It is really to help you retain and grow your existing customers AFTER you have acquired them.

Here's another dimension to the Loyalty Ladder **propounded by COLLOQUY** (the erstwhile expert knowledge base on Loyalty) many years ago. The emotional dimension.

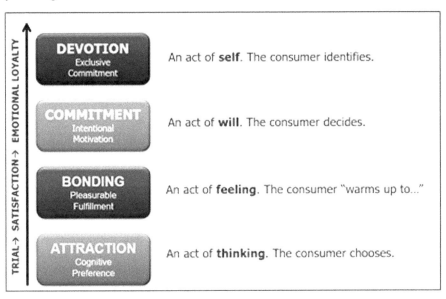

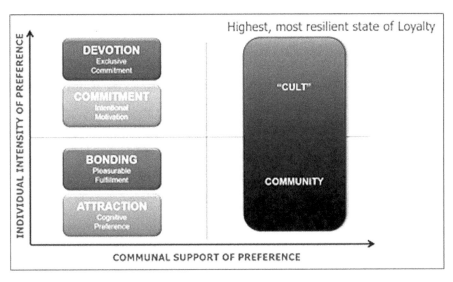

As the consumer moves from attraction to devotion, the intensity of preference increases. Switching becomes tougher. And as the brand is able to get more and more consumers to travel up this emotional ladder it is able to create a "cult" with a passionate and devoted following.

What then is LOYALTY MARKETING? And why is it important?

LOYALTY MARKETING is the marketing effort to IDENTIFY your best customers and then RETAIN and INCREASE what these customers yield to your business, by building long-term, interactive and value-added profitable relationships with them.

Let's break this down.

- First, you have to be able to **identify your best customers**. Which means you have to know who they are. They are not a faceless group. And you need to know HOW to identify them if you don't already have a mechanism to do so

- **Best customers** – those who are **valuable to you now AND those who are likely to become valuable to you in the future**. Which means you need to define what "best" is in the context of your own business. Is BEST the customer who gives you the most revenue? Is BEST the customer who transacts with you the most frequently? Is BEST the customer who has stayed with you the longest? **You** define it for your business.

- You need to **retain and increase their yield** with you. You need to grow and develop these customers. They need to STAY with you and continue buying your brand/ transacting with you

- And HOW do you do that? You **build relationships** with them. And these relationships are not short-term. They are **long-term and interactive**. It's a to and fro - not a one-way street. And they're value-added – you are consistently adding value to their lives as a brand they consume – and they are adding value to your business.

- And finally, it is **profitable relationships** we are talking about. We're not in the business of Loyalty Marketing because it's the new and hip thing to do. It is neither. It is because Loyalty Marketing results in profitable customer relationships.

WHY IS LOYALTY MARKETING IMPORTANT

Marketing itself is changing – and how! One-to-one, digital and social media add nuances and dimensions that were previously unheard of and technology has become the greatest enabler whilst parallelly lowering costs.

What are some of the changes we are seeing:

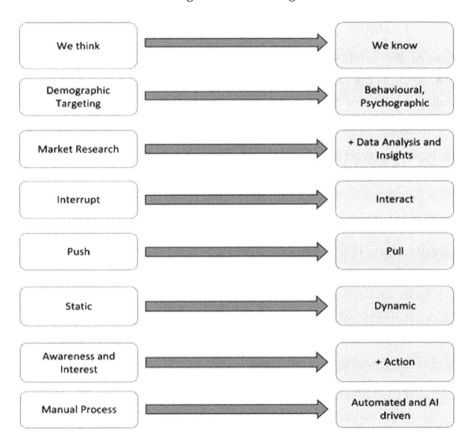

Now, more than ever, when the battle for each share point is intense, do brands need to identify whom they want to target and what behaviour they want to affect. More than ever do they need to be flexible and dynamic. More than ever do they need personalisation and customisation.

More than ever do they need Loyalty Marketing.

Loyalty Marketing has its basis in Behavioural Science. We need to believe two things:

- Some customers ARE more valuable than others and need to be treated differently. There's no two ways about this. This is not a democracy.

- Relationships with these customers CAN be managed and enabled. Behaviour CAN be modulated through these relationships.

One of the fundamental business principles that apply in Loyalty Marketing is the Pareto Principle. Vilfredo Pareto said, "…. For many outcomes, 80% of consequences come from 20% of causes…" . This is also known as the 80:20 rule.

In business, typically 80% of your profits come from 20% of your customers. While it may not be exactly 80:20, it is a fact that bulk of your profits come from a small group of core customers who need to be protected and nurtured. This is Loyalty Marketing.

Loyalty Marketing is important because:

1. It improves your customers' lifetime value with your brand
2. It improves your brand's share of the customer wallet. And customer share growth will lead to brand market share growth
3. It reduces customer churn
4. It provides a framework for relevant dialogue which actually helps achieve all of the above

DATA – THE INPUT AND THE OUTPUT

The foundation for Loyalty Marketing is therefore – DATA. It is data at a customer level that will enable the building of meaningful and long term relationships with them. And as they transact with you and relate to your brand, you know more and more about them, adding to the databank that is now becoming a powerhouse of information for you to use. So the biggest offshoot of loyalty marketing is also DATA.

WHERE IT WORKS AND WHERE IT DOESN'T

Loyalty marketing works best when:

- The environment is competitive
- There is price, product, service parity – what will distinguish brands then is the relationship they take the trouble to build with their customers
- There is perishable inventory – e.g. airlines, hotels. If you don't fill an airline seat or a hotel room for a flight/night, that inventory perishes. It is not like a washing machine that is not sold today and still remains in the showroom tomorrow.
- There is recorded customer level transaction behaviour in the course of doing business - e.g. financial services, travel, e-commerce, food tech, mobility tech
- The purchase is high value and/or high involvement
- The purchase cycle is frequent – offering more opportunities for interaction with the brand

What Loyalty Marketing can't do:

- Fix a broken business model – your brand is not distributed well. Loyalty marketing can't do much. Your brand is priced too high. Loyalty marketing is not the answer.

- Replace basics of quality, service, value. You have frequent break-downs. Fix that before you expect returns from loyalty marketing.

- Bring in new customers in double-quick time. Loyalty marketing is typically NOT for customer acquisition.

- Generate quick profits.

Loyalty marketing is not a quick-fix solution. It takes time, effort, consistency and commitment. And it pays-off. **It's not that hard!**

CHAPTER 2

TYPES OF LOYALTY INITIATIVES

"Would you tell me, please, which way I ought to go from here?'
'That depends a good deal on where you want to get to,' said the
Cat. Alice In Wonderland

We're now going to take a look at the options before us when we start on the journey of Loyalty Marketing.

You're browsing online on an e-commerce site. Looking at stuff that perhaps interests you. Or aimlessly surfing. The e-com site however believes that you must be interested because you took the trouble to visit them. And let's say you've registered on the site with your email id. You will most likely start getting multiple mails urging you to go back and complete your selection.

Or you buy something online on Amazon. The website now has your email id and most likely your mobile number too. You start getting mails, messages, WhatsApps – thank you for shopping, your item is on its way etc etc – and also, here's something else that might interest you. Amazon may now tell you to subscribe to Prime if you're not already a member.

You order Domino's Pizza online or on the phone. You start getting offers on long weekends, on new toppings, on a totally new pizza or side option.

You're a Shoppers Stop First Citizen Club member. You shop at the store (or online) - when you check out, they know you're a member, they ask you if you want to redeem points, they may ask you to validate your parking ticket if any.

You're flying Air Vistara. You're a Club Vistara Platinum member. At the airport you get a separate check-in queue, lounge facility and priority boarding and baggage.

Fundamentally, all of the above are examples of attempting to build a relationship with your existing and prospective customers. The form they take is, however, different.

Let's start with the basic difference. The e-commerce sites and Domino's are marketing to you as a customer whose data they have. Not as **a loyalty program member**. Shoppers Stop and Vistara however, are building a relationship with their Loyalty Program members. The first is what we call COVERT Loyalty Marketing and the Second is OVERT Loyalty Marketing.

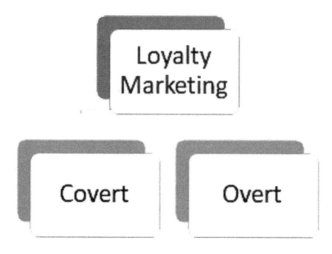

COVERT INITIATIVES:

These are CRM initiatives using customer data that is collected as a process of doing business. The brand has not "announced" any loyalty program, the customers are not "members". But they're still targeting you (hopefully relevantly; sadly, however, often as a mass outreach) based on the data they have about you - your contact details and your transactions (browsing history for online shopping) at the very least. Based on this, they send you messages, offers and deals. They trigger next behaviour like the second transaction or purchase of another category. There are several examples of brands that follow this. Many automobile brands follow this. Most banks and financial services do this. E commerce sites are masters at this. Travel brands sometimes do this as well.

Covert initiatives operate "under the radar" so to speak. The customer is not made obviously aware that his/her behaviour is being tracked, analysed and used for marketing - though consent to use data is always taken. At the back-end, it is based on segmentation and targeted messaging with relevant content and offers. To that extent, the customer has no expectations from the brand in terms of delivery.

A caveat here is that today's online shoppers are savvy. They know they have allowed themselves to be tracked when they shop – and they expect their data to be used responsibly and effectively.

Many brands consciously choose to build customer relationships only with covert CRM initiatives. **There are many advantages to this:**

1. When customer expectations are lower, there is lower pressure on delivery on-the-ground

2. The technology to manage the CRM back-end is simpler than having a complete loyalty system – and hence, quicker to get off the ground

3. There is minimal dependence on frontline staff – it's all centrally controlled

4. Lower investments required

5. With sufficient relevance and added dollops of surprise and delight, CRM initiatives prove effective in building relationships

So – simpler, quicker and less investment-intensive. But, as with anything, it's not all rosy. Else, why would we have such successful loyalty programs running for brands!

Some of the pitfalls to watch out for:

- The customer is less invested because they are not "members", they don't "belong". They are passive passengers in the exercise. So they're naturally less committed to the brand and the initiative – unless the brand itself commands powerful equity. E.g. Apple has no program. Walmart in the US had no program until recently - hinging their whole proposition on the EDLP (Every Day Low Prices). Domino's India started a loyalty program called the Upper Crust but called it off a couple of years down the line, relying on its CRM entirely. They have, recently, gone back to an Overt Initiative called Cheesy Rewards.

- There is no "tangible offering" – like points or miles or stars. Hence, no accrual, less stickiness. And again, less customer "investment" in the brand.

- While there is a distinctive tone and manner that reflects the brand, there is no equity created by a branded entity like a loyalty program and its tiers, its currency.

OVERT INITIATIVES

Some brands choose to go with overt and announced initiatives to build customer loyalty. They announce a "program", customers are solicited for membership into the program, and all loyalty initiatives are run under the ambit of this program.

There is a PROGRAM BRAND; if the program has a currency then there is a branding for the CURRENCY (XYZ Points, Miles, Smiles, Stars); if there are tiers then there are TIER NAMES too.

There is a clear positioning and identity for the program, with a stated value proposition on offer.

What are such programs that you can think of? About 5 years ago, two names would stand out in any India research on Loyalty. Jet Privilege and Shoppers Stop First Citizen. Jet Privilege has, since then, become Intermiles. There are, of course, many more we can think of spontaneously today. Marriott Bonvoy. Titan Encircle. Club Vistara. Flipkart SuperCoins. Taj Inner Circle. Club ITC. Payback. Levi's Loop. Arrow Aristocracy. And of course, Tata Neu – which today subsumes all Tata group company programs including Taj and Titan. Amazon Prime - yes, that too.

There are several advantages of overt initiatives:

1. Strong branding opportunity and recall

2. Customer "investment" in the program as they are members and feel a sense of belonging. This results in higher business payoffs

3. This is a tangible offering that the customer/member can very easily vocalize – "Yes the brand has a program that gives me special service and points"

4. If there is currency, it accrues and provides stickiness. There is a tendency to consolidate earnings with one brand.

5. Demonstrable commitment from the brand to the customer. The fact that the brand is putting time, resources and investments behind this, is tangible proof to the customers that they're serious about building customer relationships.

6. Most importantly, where data is not already captured as part of the transaction, this is the best way to capture data. The

moment customers enrol, you start getting to know more about them.

However, things to bear in mind:

1. It takes dedication and commitment for the long term. Once launched, an overt initiative cannot be shut down at will. It means you have to invest in it, and continue to invest in it – even if you are not breaking even in the first couple of years. It takes a leap of faith to believe that it WILL pay off handsomely to make it all worthwhile in the not-too-distant future.

2. It immediately pegs customer expectations higher and puts pressure on delivery. If I am a program member, I immediately feel special and want the brand to treat me so. This means organisation-wide training, customer-facing staff orientation and refreshers, in-store elements of differentiation for retail brands etc.

3. There are investments of time and resources required to set it up - the loyalty system, integration with existing technology and legacy systems, related infrastructure including member services, teams to run the program, frontline delivery etc. It takes time to get it off the ground. You want action immediately? An overt loyalty program is not the answer.

4. Resulting therefore in higher costs, higher risks. And yes, higher returns too.

HISTORY OF OVERT LOYALTY INITIATIVES

Loyalty programs are actually as old as brands and advertising. The period from 1850 - 1980 was rife with what was called Continuity Programs – Cigarette cards, trading stamps. Who doesn't remember Ramon Bonus Stamps? How many remember the Binaca toys with every toothpaste pack? Every Pepsi Lays packet had something called a Tazo. Tazos were collected avidly by children, gloated over, traded.

All these were techniques to drive repeat purchase and build loyalty, though no data was collected.

The "birth" of modern loyalty programs is ascribed to American Airlines AAdvantage in 1981. With the US deregulation of airlines in 1978, competition exploded and fares declined. There was pressure on airlines to retain their best customers. American Airlines led the way with the first "Loyalty Program" that used customer data (reservation system) to track behaviour, had a currency for the first time and had soft benefits (upgrades) as a key ingredient.

After that, Loyalty Marketing Programs spread in concentric circles outwards from the airline industry. United Airlines followed AA. And then Marriott launched its Honored Guest program in 1983 followed by Neiman Marcus launching InCircle in 1984. Thereafter, there was no looking back.

Today loyalty programs are ubiquitous. 84% of US adults belong to at least one program with memberships growing at 15% p.a. The Wise Marketer (an authority on Customer Loyalty) estimates that the global market for loyalty program memberships is at 5 Billion+ with an activity rate of 70%!

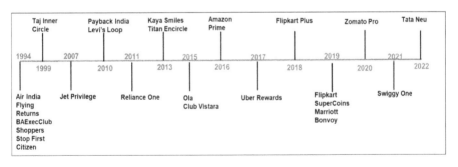

Closer home, let's look at the history of modern loyalty marketing in India.

Starting in 1994 with Air India Flying Returns and Shoppers Stop First Citizen, programs have now made a presence in all verticals, including new age food tech and mobility tech.

The India Loyalty Program Market *(as per the Future Market Insights report 2022)* is estimated to top nearly USD 3364 Mn in 2023 and reach USD 14500 Mn in 2033 at a CAGR of 15.7%. India is believed to hold 4-8% of the global loyalty market.

Covert or Overt – there's no getting away from building stronger relationships with your customers. And... it's not that hard!

CHAPTER 3

PROGRAM MODELS

Sometimes the right path is not the easiest one... Pocahontas

When a brand decides to launch a branded, OVERT loyalty initiative, there are several program business models to choose from. And this will be one of the first strategic decisions to take when designing for loyalty.

Let's now look at an overview of different program models and the pros and cons of each. There are no rights or wrongs, the task is to choose the best fit for your business and your objectives at the time.

Program models discussed are not mutually exclusive or exhaustive. Brands have chosen to operate multiple models at a time or a combination of different models depending on the brand objectives at that point in time.

PROPRIETARY MODEL

Bata Club. Starbucks Rewards. Nykaa Prive. Club Vistara. IKEA Family. FabFamily.

Gap Good Rewards. Nordstrom Nordy Club. Harrod's Rewards.

These are some examples of PROPRIETARY loyalty programs. When a brand launches an overt loyalty program for its customers, entirely owned and controlled by the brand, it is a Proprietary program. The program centres around the brand - the value proposition is what is offered by the brand to its customers. If there is a program currency, it is earned and redeemed on the brand purchases/brand catalogue. The program cost centre is within the brand and resultant risks and profits are held by the brand.

There was a time when most overt initiatives started out as proprietary programs though that's not the case anymore.

Programs not mentioned here – Shoppers Stop First Citizen, Jet Privilege, Tanishq Anuttara – started off as proprietary programs – and were hugely successful.

There are many advantages to launching a proprietary program:

1. The brand has complete control over the program value proposition. It can ensure that it dovetails seamlessly with brand objectives, tone and manner and culture.

2. Being in sole control, the brand can also tweak, even change, the value proposition when the situation demands it. Flexibility is a huge plus.

3. There is complete ownership of program data within the brand ecosystem

4. This data can be leveraged effectively and it becomes a competitive edge for the brand. The powerhouse of data creates value far in excess of cost.

5. The program brand enhances the parent brand – especially for successful programs.

As with any thing, there are risks and constraints to keep in mind:

1. The program is a cost centre before it becomes a profit centre. That is a reality. The brand must have the financial muscle,

commitment and wherewithal to stay the course and run the program

2. There are capital investments to be made – in technology and infrastructure

3. The risks of poor design and poor implementation fall solely on the brand which then has to bear the consequences

4. It is, in fact, the most expensive model to operate and maintain

5. It takes considerable time to get it off the ground and running.

PARTNER MODEL

Shoppers Stop First Citizen. Flipkart SuperCoins. Most airline programs. Marriott Bonvoy.

Proprietary programs often extend into Partner Programs. In order to enhance the value proposition, the brand ropes in PARTNERS for its program.

The program **ownership** is still with the brand, data is still centrally held with the brand, the branding and currency remain the brand's. Partners are brought in to add value, variety and velocity.

The relationship that the program has with partners will vary and will depend on the agreement with the partner.

Partners could be:

- Earn partners – the program currency can be earned at partner outlets too. Once the Jet Privilege program had stabilised, it had tied up partners like restaurants etc where JP members could go and earn Jet Miles for their spend.

- Burn partners – the program currency can be redeemed against purchases at a partner outlet

- Earn and Burn partners – partners sign an agreement where both earn and burn is allowed at their outlets.

- Tactical Partners/Promotional partners – partner brands make special offers to the program member base (or some segments of the program member base). This could be in the form of standing offers (for a specified period, or not specified) where a program member walks in to a partner outlet and is entitled to a free drink/ 10% off etc. Or it could be a set of offers/vouchers from complementary brands that is offered by a program to its members.

Co-branded cards that some loyalty programs offer, are also a type of Partnership. Let's take the example of the Shoppers Stop HDFC Bank co-branded card. When a member uses this card, he/she earns double the points at Shoppers Stop (a portion being funded by the bank) and also earns points on the card being used elsewhere like a normal credit card. The burn (redemption) of these points however can happen only at Shoppers Stop.

Essentially a Partner Model means:

1. Ownership is still centralised with the originating brand

2. An enhanced value proposition – no longer does it centre only around the parent brand

3. An enhanced database – because there is some view of spend outside of the brand – though what data is shared depends on consent taken and agreement with partner brands

4. There is a broader dialogue with members beyond transactions at and relationship with the parent brand

There are several advantages of this:

1. The enhanced proposition adds value to members and to the brand – especially so if the primary brand does not have enough variety and velocity of purchase to offer on its own. Roping in partners means leveraging OPM – Other People's Money.

2. Richer data collection and shared relationships with control still in the hands of the parent brand

3. Program now becomes a profit centre on its own. Especially so if there is a currency and there is a buy and sell rate of currency agreed upon with partners

4. Competitive advantage as long as exclusivity agreements are signed

Risks and cautions to remember:

1. If partners are not selected carefully (even the tactical and short-term partners), there is risk of dilution to the parent brand. I can think of several examples of payment, telecom and digital providers who offer a series of vouchers on usage, renewals and recharges. How many of those are even useable and what value do they add to your perception of the brand offering the same?

2. Take care to see that there is synergy between your brand and partner brands in terms of target audience. There is a ubiquity of brands today who are on the prowl for customer acquisition and partnering with existing programs to make offers is a simple way for them. It is up to the program brand to be discerning.

3. The cost and risk is still that of the parent brand

4. If the experience and recognition is not delivered at the partner outlets, the backlash falls squarely on the program, not the partner brand.

Today, many programs are launched as partner programs because brands are conscious of the fact that Gen Y, Gen Z, Gen Alpha all seek variety and novelty - and this is great way of creating a holistic proposition.

PLAYER MODEL

A Player Model is essentially the inverse of the Partner model. Some brands consciously choose not to launch their own programs for various reasons. Either they feel the brand cannot sustain variety and velocity of the program on its own, the costs are too high, they don't want to take the risk individually or they don't want to undergo the hassle of setting up the whole program infrastructure. Yet, they feel the need to build loyalty with their customer base.

What do they do? They choose to PLAY in someone else's program. When Jet Miles could be earned at Rajdhani Restaurants, Jet Privilege was a PARTNER program but Rajdhani Restaurants had adopted a PLAYER program model. They were PLAYING in the Jet Privilege program.

The player brand reaps benefits from this strategy:

1. It gains an entry into loyalty without much initial investment

2. Suddenly, the brand now has a proposition to offer beyond what it can sustain on its own. Imagine, if you will, a small brand starting to offer Flipkart SuperCoins against purchase. The brand now becomes part of a larger eco system and customers start seeing the benefit.

3. It is a quick start – not much prep time required

4. Data pay-offs of loyalty start flowing in – though it depends on the agreement with the program owner.

What are the possible disadvantages?

1. The relationship with the member is second-hand. The primary relationship is held by the program brand owner

2. There may not be much branding rub-off for the player brand.

3. The player brand has no control over the program proposition – it literally plays in a field that is already set

When brands have the equity, the strength of offering and the financial wherewithal to have their own program, they would prefer to do that vs playing in someone else's program

COALITION MODEL

Payback. Tata Neu. Titan Encircle. Air Miles. Nectar. Zillion. Reliance One.

And this is the biggie. Though still trying to find its feet in India......

Picture this. There is an independent entity that is set up to launch a program. The entity is the program owner and the currency owner. It is also the data and customer "owner". It then sets about tying in various partners (SPONSORS) to become part of this program. So you get a grocery retailer, a bank, a telecom operator, an airline, a utility provider, a specialty retailer, a hotel chain all becoming SPONSORS in the program. This is your textbook COALITION program.

Each sponsor has an arm's length distance from the program owning entity. They are however part of the overall proposition on offer to the customer and they issue and/or redeem the program's currency.

Agreements with Sponsors are carefully drafted and watertight. There will be category exclusivity clauses, tenures and partnership levels (including equity stake in the ownership entity) specified and earn-burn rates of currency also pre-defined.

How is this different from Shoppers Stop roping in partners for the First Citizen Program? In that case, Shoppers Stop is the still the program and currency owning entity – there is no arm's length distance. And partners play in the playing field set by Shoppers Stop.

There are two or three broad Coalition formats:

1. Tata Neu is, right now, a CLOSED COALITION. It is a Coalition of all Tata Group Companies. Tata Digital owns the program and most Tata brands are part of it. Titan Encircle likewise was a Closed Coalition of all Titan Companies. It has

now been subsumed into Tata Neu. In India, where we have large business conglomerates across industries and verticals, Closed Coalitions are a fairly obvious solution. Reliance One, similarly, is a Coalition of Reliance Companies. Expect to see a Mahindra & Mahindra coalition at some point. The same is true of the Middle East. Large business conglomerates in the Gulf operate their own closed Coalitions. Shukran from the Landmark group is an example.

2. Zillion – erstwhile Payback India - is an OPEN COALITION. Bharat Pe owns the independent entity – with ownership transferred multiple times (iMint from ICICI, then Payback Germany, then Amex, and now currently Bharat Pe) and the program has a set of sponsors across categories.

3. You may also have Coalitions targeted at a specific audience (teens, seniors citizens, veterans, college grads) or a specific geography (e.g. A Bengaluru based Coalition with local retailers) – Coalition Lites, as they are called in the U.S

Coalitions work like this:

-   The "owning" entity owns the program, currency, data and customer

-   They handle the branding and marketing of the program as a whole

-   Each sponsor is given data pertaining to transactions with their respective brands.

-   Data and MIS reports on aggregate behaviour and insights thereof are shared with all partners

-   Each sponsor will be given *access* to the member base to market their brand – with clearly defined terms and conditions.

-   Sponsors who issue currency will "buy" the currency at a specified, pre-agreed rate from the owning entity.

- Sponsors who redeem currency will be compensated for redeemed currency at a pre-agreed rate (normally lower than the issuing rate) by the owning entity

- The earn-burn rate arbitrage is where the Coalition earns its margins

- Revenues are collected on issuance (not adjusted as net of redemption) and positive cash flows are a sign of success of a coalition.

- Other revenue streams for the Coalition entity include

  - Charges for exclusivity

  - Commitment on currency purchased for issuance in a specified period

  - Data sharing with partners

  - Marketing of sponsor brands at specified rates

  - Charging a rental for "real estate" on all program communication – media sales

  - MIS and reporting services

- Coalitions need to be fair to all participating sponsors – though agreement with each sponsor is individually drafted

The advantages of a Coalition:

1. Brands become part of a larger eco system that has its own momentum and traction – assuming the Coalition is marketed well

2. There is a sharing of costs and infrastructure

3. Data view outside of own brand – at aggregate level. And deep insights of transactions at their own brand.

4. Great customer acquisition vehicle – members will start buying brands that are part of the Coalition just to consolidate and

accelerate their earnings. Coalition is one loyalty model that actually plays a role in acquisition too – not just in retention

The risks:

1. A Coalition that is just starting takes a long, long – really long – time to get off the ground!

2. Agreements and exclusivity can be tricky – difficult to manoeuvre

3. And, like the partner model, the relationship is second hand. Loyalty is being built to the Coalition, not to individual brands - unless sponsor brands actually take the trouble, time and investment to use this opportunity and data window to build equity for their respective brands.

CURRENCY EXCHANGE MODEL

A very quick look at another model that is quite popular in Europe and will soon make its way here. The Currency Exchange Model.

This is really the way Proprietary and Partner programs evolve. Essentially the individual program currency is fungible and can be EXCHANGED with other program currencies. Either this is done with individual (principal to principal) agreements between two programs – or it actually happens on an Exchange platform – much like a market currency exchange. The rate that each program currency commands on buy and sell then depends on market dynamics and the power of the currency.

This is as yet new to India and we will wait for the scenario to develop.

CHOOSING THE BEST MODEL

Each program model option has its pros and cons. There are no absolute right or wrong answers. It depends on where your brand is in the loyalty journey and what the organisation objectives are.

Each model serves different objectives:

OBJECTIVES	PROPRIETARY	PARTNER	PLAYER	COALITION
Gain individual customer data				
Understanding shopping habits beyond your brand				
Acquire customers				
Easy to change value proposition				
Limit cost/financial risk				
Enhance your brand				
Differentiate from competition				
Create a profit centre				

Choosing YOUR model would be a factor of:

1. Organisation and Brand objectives
2. Economics and financial considerations
3. Current customer equity
4. Market dynamics
5. Competitive scenario
6. Long term view

A quick overview of the different Overt Loyalty Program models is a precursor to the process of designing an Overt Loyalty initiative. The book will now get into a step-by-step description of designing a loyalty program and getting it off the ground.

It's not that hard!

CHAPTER 4

PROGRAM DESIGN PROCESS AND DISCOVERY

"The best way to explain it is to do it" The Dodo,
Alice in Wonderland

Loyalty program design follows a systematic process. It is important to seamlessly integrate with overall organisation goals and not plan for loyalty as a silo operating on its own.

Typically, the program design process follows what we call the 3D approach:

Essentially it comprises:

1. Going through the process of Discovery to understand the landscape and creating a framework for loyalty marketing – DISCOVER

2. Getting into the details of program design, value proposition, structure, features, rules and modelling – DESIGN

3. Setting down a blueprint for implementation – DEVELOP

There are specific inputs and outputs for each stage of the 3D Approach

Discover	Design	Develop

•Input
  •Business, Environment,
   Customer understanding
•Output
  •Objectives Prioritised
  •Opportunities and
   Constraints
  •Guardrails and framework
   for design
	•Input
	  •Discovery findings
	  •Data analysis
	•Output
	  •Program Design detailing
	  •Program Structure
	  •Program Metrics and
	   Measurement
	  •Program Financial Model
		•Input
		  •Program Design document
		   and rule book
		•Output
		  •Program Implementation
		   requirements and timelines
		  •Program activity and
		   communication calendar
		  •Program partnership and
		   rewards plan

DISCOVERY

The real voyage of Discovery consists not in seeking new landscapes, but in having new eyes – *Marcel Proust*

Discovery is the first stage in the program design process. If you don't understand where you are, you can't plan where you want to go and how to get there.

The Discovery process involves understanding the organisation and the landscape within which it operates. A good approach is to structure the information sought in the form of concentric circles moving from inside to outside

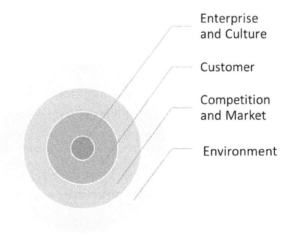

Enterprise and Culture

Customer

Competition and Market

Environment

1. ENTERPRISE AND CULTURE

The first step is to understand the Organisation and the environment it operates within. This will require information search in the following areas:

- Organisation
    - Organisation vision, goals and objectives, performance
    - Organisation Structure
    - Organisation Culture (explore independence of decision-making unit, risk appetite, aggressiveness, accountability), alignment, readiness for loyalty
- What has sparked the need for loyalty, what are the expectations from Loyalty
- Audience
    - Target audience definition – demographics and lifestyle indicators
    - Primary and Secondary audiences
    - Users, Influencers and Decision makers
- Product and Marketing
    - Product lines, brand architecture and expansion plans, brand values and positioning
    - Marketing initiatives – above and below the line - and their impact, effectiveness
    - Organisation's view of competition (who do they view as competition and what is their view on competitive strengths, weaknesses, initiatives)
- Sales and Distribution
    - Sales and distribution structure and related financials (margins etc)
    - Sales growth trends

- Financials and Viability
  - Costs, budgets, allowables (how much is the organisation willing to spend on loyalty initiatives)
  - Where is the funding for loyalty likely to come from? Margins? Marketing Expenditure? Promotions and Discounts Budget? Product Lines?
- Technology and infrastructure
  - Technology and infrastructure in existence – and planned for
  - What existing systems can be leveraged
- Other areas specific to the organisation

Typically, the information is gathered over the period of a few weeks and will involve:

- **Stakeholder workshops/interviews with key stakeholders across functions** – Loyalty initiatives have the greatest chance of success when they are driven top down AND bottom up in the organisation. When there is a commitment from the CEO's office, then there is a seriousness to the design process. Stakeholder workshops will be held with the CxO office (focus on vision and goals, why loyalty), Marketing, Sales and Distribution, Finance, Legal, IT, Field staff, Outlet staff – and others who may be specific to the Organisation. Workshops are typically held as half-day sessions with discussions around specific areas following a structured discussion guide. **A key area of debate will be the expectations from Loyalty** – one would normally find that expectations are different across different functions and it is important to map these down and arrive at a common agenda in terms of what loyalty will deliver. Couple of probing questions to consider: **"What is the single metric that will make you say that the loyalty initiative is a success?"** Or conversely **"What is the single indicator for you that the Loyalty initiative has not worked?"**. While it is always difficult to gather all stakeholders in a single room, try and have at least one common session where objectives are frozen. This is critical for alignment later.

- **Study of existing relevant material** in the system- documents and presentations, research reports, campaign analysis reports, brand manuals etc

- **Technical mapping of current infrastructure**, system specifications etc so that recommendations later are not out of whack with what already exists.

- **Desk research on Best Practices** – to supplement information gathered in specific areas like infrastructure and technology options, data privacy regulations (a big one today), structuring the organisation for Loyalty

As a starting point for Enterprise Discovery:

- It is useful to first identify WHO the key stakeholders are and then prepare discussion guides for each forthcoming conversation.

- It is also useful to prepare a list of INFORMATION NEEDS by department/function and then collate the information and supporting documents received based on that.

CUSTOMER

Customer Discovery will seek to answer three questions:

- Who is the customer?
- How are customers behaving?
- Why are they behaving like this?

The answers to these questions will come from two sources:

- **Data Analysis : Data is almost a "must" requirement as an input for loyalty program design.** Typically, the discovery process would involve slicing and dicing of 24-36 months of transaction data at a customer level. This will help answer questions on:

- What customer segments are emerging – who are the most and least valuable, who are the vulnerable ones

- What are the key transaction metrics – Avg Transaction Value (ATV), Frequency, Basket size and composition

- What are the emerging trends in behaviour

- What are the gaps and opportunity areas

A detailed chapter on data analysis for Loyalty Program Design follows later in the book.

In the absence of customer-level transaction data, the analysis would use other data available in the system - e.g. store level data, bill data, sales data, online transaction data, even conversations with key stakeholders on the metrics - as indicators to draw some conclusions. Very often there are hidden treasures of information within the organisation that most are not even aware of. The loyalty discovery process helps unearth these and put them to good use.

Data analysis is a key ingredient of program design – any data adds to the information even if perfect data is not available. The quest is not for perfection. The quest is for direction and insights.

What data analysis tells you is – WHAT customers are doing with your brand. It does not tell you WHY.

- **Hence the importance of the second arm of customer-related information – RESEARCH.** A digestion of all customer research available in the system will be the starting point. It tells you who the customers are, what their attitudes and perceptions are towards your brand, perhaps their intentions of using your brand in future, their satisfactions and dissatisfactions with the brand.

This is then supplemented with additional research that is geared specifically towards loyalty. Research as an input into loyalty design is not necessarily large sample and quantitative. A caveat here is that quantitative research can be used as a good indicator of surrogate metrics when transaction data at a customer level is not available.

Qualitative interviews and focus groups are a great way of gleaning insights into habits and purchase behaviour, barriers to purchase, view of competitive brands (from the horses' mouths so to speak), intentions and satisfactions – and, most importantly, expectations from loyalty. As part of research, it is useful to plot a **DILO – Day in the Life Of** – the target customer. This tool gives huge insights into what drives the customer and where and how best to reach her with the relevant messaging.

There will be a section dedicated entirely to familiarity with loyalty programs, likes and dislikes, anecdotal evidence (very important to build a value proposition) and expectations from your brand in terms of loyalty including specifics on rewards, recognition, services and privileges which will be important ingredients of the value proposition.

Tools that are useful for Customer Discovery are:

- Research plan and Discussion guide for research
- Data Audit
- Data Analysis Plan

3. COMPETITION AND MARKET

Loyalty program design, as with any marketing initiative, cannot be done in the absence of a competitive view. It is important to know about the following:

- **Direct competitive brands** – which are these brands and what are they doing for the customer, how does your brand stack up, what are the competitive advantages and weaknesses, what is the "white space" in the category that can be leveraged

- **Indirect competition** – brands that may not be in the same vertical, but will compete for the same share of the customer's wallet. E.g. entertainment could compete for the same share of wallet as F&B/ Dining. And what are these indirect competition brands doing? What are the category dynamics that influence choice of category?

- **Market initiatives** – trade practices prevalent, promotions that are common (e.g. twice a year EOSS – End of Season Sale – in apparel retail), is outsourcing to franchisees common, is discounting a regular practice, how common are loyalty programs etc

- **Brands targeting the same audience even if different categories** – e.g. Luxury Hospitality and Premium Apparel – what are they doing

- **Loyalty Marketing Best Practices** – in India and Globally - same audience, same category, outstanding examples that may work across categories and audiences

A multi-pronged effort is required to get this information:

- **Stakeholder workshops** will give the inside out view – detailed conversations with marketing, sales and distribution personnel will help give a perspective on the market status

- **Market visits** – ideally choose strong and weak markets for the brand – visit the markets, visit the outlets of brand and competition, speak to field staff and outlet staff, speak to customers in-store - nothing really paints a picture as visiting the market yourself. Market visits also give insights into competitive loyalty programs and how they are operating. Enrol into competitive programs to better get a view of how the actual member journey looks like, what the program responsiveness is etc.

- **Desk Research and Benchmarking** - Extensive desk research is required especially on loyalty best practices. It is useful to create a templated format across which one compares different loyalty programs – and create separate worksheets for India vs Global programs for easier comparison. Typically, programs are compared across features like : eligibility, enrolment process, tiering, program earn and burn, program services, program benefits and privileges etc.

Input tools to structure Competition and Market Discovery:

- Benchmarking Template worksheets
- Market/Field visit plan with supporting Discussion Guides for all conversations to be had during the field visits
- Competition Mapping template/grid/matrix

ENVIRONMENT

Any Discovery has to bear in mind the Environment and context within which the Enterprise is functioning and the loyalty initiative is being designed.

Specific questions to be answered here include:

- How is the overall economy doing and are there threats of a slowdown?
- What are the environment challenges that we will have to deal with?
- What are the regulatory considerations specific to the industry? E.g. E Commerce has specific regulations in India, FDI regulations in multi-brand retail, regulations for use of surrogates in promotion of brands in specific industries like alcohol and tobacco, healthcare dos and don'ts

- Are there any new entrants expected – or product substitutes?
- What are the developments in related areas of Digital, Social, Payments, Technology, Mobile ?

Normally information on the Environment comes from

- Stakeholder workshops
- Desk research
- Expert interviews with experts in the relevant fields

DISCOVERY PHASE OUTPUT/DELIVERABLES

The objective of conducting a detailed Discovery process is to set a realistic context and framework for the Loyalty Program design.

Having understood the contours of ECCE, there are key output deliverables which then become the touchstone of reference for the next phase – Design.

1. Stakeholder Workshops report - will summarise the key takeaways from each stakeholder interview/workshop conducted. This will help identify and prioritise objectives for loyalty, gaps and constraints, opportunity areas

2. Customer Research Report – key takeaways from existing research as well as qualitative research conducted for loyalty

3. Data Analysis Report – segmentation, MVCs, high potential customers, behaviour that is to be rewarded and recognised, key transaction metrics, headroom for growth

4. Competition Mapping and Benchmarking report - white space and differentiation areas

5. Best Practices Benchmarking Report – learnings and possible adaptations

6. Environment Scan Report – guardrails for loyalty framework

7. Loyalty Framework

The Discovery phase normally takes about 6-8 weeks depending on the availability of key stakeholders for inputs. The exploration of ECCE elements will normally start in parallel after an initial kick-off and overview with the primary stakeholder and FPOC.

Once the seven deliverables are in place, we are now ready to get into the Design phase of the program.

And yes, it's not that hard!

CHAPTER 5

ELEMENTS OF PROGRAM DESIGN

OBJECTIVES AND STRATEGY

"I must go <u>forward</u> where I have never been instead of backwards where I have." Winnie The Pooh

We are now embarking on the Program Design phase.

After 6-8 weeks of Discovery we have set the guardrails and program framework. We have understood the brand and its priorities. We are now ready to get into the different elements of Program Design.

Before we get into a detailed understanding of each with examples and illustrations, let us understand what we will cover:

1. Setting Objectives – Based on the Discovery Output we arrive at a priority of objectives for the loyalty initiative. These are cast in stone – at least for the short and medium term.

2. Value Proposition – Once we know what the program needs to achieve, we carefully craft and curate a Program Value Proposition

3. Eligibility and Enrolment – We define rules around who is eligible for the program and how we will enrol them

4. Free or Fee – A crucial decision on whether the program is free or whether a fee should be charged. You guessed right – there are pros and cons for both!

5. Membership and Renewal – we then get into the conditions around membership and renewal

6. Currency Principles – if the value proposition specifies that there is a program currency – then what is the currency strategy and what are the principles around currency management

7. Tiering – will the program have tiers and what are the rules around tiering

8. Rewards and Redemption – perhaps the biggest moment of truth in loyalty. What kind of rewards does the program offer and what is the redemption process. This will also get into the details of what kind of recognition, services, benefits and privileges the program will offer.

And once we are done with this, we have a program in place that will then be subject to the rigors of financial modelling.

Remember that each step links with the previous and must lead to the next. And all must be geared to deliver on the program objectives.

SETTING PROGRAM OBJECTIVES

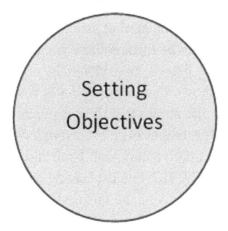

This is the initial and most critical step in design. When we go through stakeholder workshops during Discovery, we often find that each department and function will have different priorities and expectations from the loyalty initiative. We will end up getting varying objectives. The loyalty initiative will almost seem like a magic wand that is there to solve all the business issues with one flourishing sweep!

Our task is then two-fold:

1. Focus

2. Clarity

We first sift through all the expectations, put them into logical groups and view them in the light of all the other information collected during Discovery. This brings FOCUS on what is the priority objective. The next step is to break it down in a manner that is clear and actionable. **And remember that this is in the context of what loyalty can and should tackle.**

Let's see how this is done.

1. **PRIORITISING OBJECTIVES** – Let's say a large organisation, a market leader, is tussling with two issues – it has to protect **market share** fiercely. It also has to figure out how to grow the **market size** to meet evolving customer needs. This may be through new geographies, new product variants, new brands, new channels, other innovations etc. Discovery shows that competition is intense and biting at the heels. It also shows that there is much to be done to meet customer expectations even at current levels. The priority for the loyalty initiative may well be to focus on the MARKET SHARE PROTECTION whilst leaving new initiatives to other areas and functions of the business. So you have a FOCUS now. **Protect Market Share**. But this is a Business Objective. Not a Loyalty Objective. Let's understand the difference.

2. **LAYERING OBJECTIVES** – When arriving at Objectives, the next step is to DIFFERENTIATE and LAYER them. There are three layers we look at and each one has to feed in to the one above:

Business Objective
• What is the Organisation's Goal?

Loyalty Objective
• How can the Loyalty Initiative contribute towards achieving the above goal?

Behaviour Objective
• What customer behaviour must driven/changed in order to achieve the loyalty objective

- **BUSINESS OBJECTIVE -** What is the Organisation's goal or objective. In the above example the Priority Business Objective is to Protect Market Share. There could be Business Objectives expressed as GROWTH, as PROFITABILITY, as EXPANSION. It could also be "social" objectives like DRIVE SUSTAINABILITY. It could be to BUILD THE CUSTOMER ASSET. PROTECT AND GROW CORE CATEGORY.

- **LOYALTY OBJECTIVE -** How can a Loyalty Objective contribute towards attaining the priority business objective. Let's continue with the example of PROTECT MARKET SHARE. What must a loyalty initiative do? It must drive retention of most valuable customers. It must drive retention and development of mid segment customers. That is what will deliver greatest impact to market share - the most valuable customers continue to remain and spend with the brand; those who are one level lower not only stay, they also start spending more. This will compensate for the churn amongst lower value customers. So we have two Loyalty Objectives

  - Retention of Most Valuable Customers (top deciles)

  - Retention and Growth of Mid Value Customers (mid deciles)

- **BEHAVIOUR OBJECTIVE -** The final layer. What specific BEHAVIOURS do we need to drive to achieve the Loyalty Objectives. What do you want the target audience to DO?

Let's assume a new loyalty initiative is being launched with the above objectives.

Here are the behaviours that we need to drive:

- **MVCs**
  - ☐ Must Opt in to the initiative
  - ☐ Must continue to visit/transact
  - ☐ Must continue to buy what they're already buying
  - ☐ Must not churn
- **Mid Segments**
  - ☐ Must Opt in to the initiative
  - ☐ Must visit more often
  - ☐ Must try new SKUs, new range
  - ☐ Must premiumise (buy higher value)

The key to setting well-defined objectives is not just focus and clarity. It is also in the articulation. The better you articulate, the more fine-tuned your strategy will be.

These are 5 Building Blocks as a guideline for better articulation:

- **WHAT -** frequency, spend, range, churn, engagement etc
- **WHERE -** which channels, which touchpoints
- **HOW MUCH -** increase, decrease, maintain
- **WHEN -** what time period
- **WHO -** what target segment

How would we better articulate the Loyalty and Behaviour objectives in the above examples

- Top 5% of our customer base must opt-in to our initiative and transact x times a year giving us a value of y across online and offline channels over the next 12 months.

- We should be able to reduce the churn of Top 5 % of our customer base by 20% over the next 12 months

OBJECTIVES VS STRATEGY

We now come to the difference between the oft-confused terms – **Objectives and Strategy.**

In definition it is a simple difference – Objective is WHAT you want to do. Strategy is HOW you will do it.

So, a loyalty objective cannot be "to recognise and reward high value customers". Nor can it be "To create an exclusive club for our customers". These are the "Hows" to achieving something.

It can be: *Top 5% of our customer base must opt-in to our initiative and transact x times a year giving us a value of y across online and offline channels over the next 12 months.*

It can also be: **Create a strong brand preference amongst members such that we become the first choice.**

Or it can be: **Drive strong emotional engagement with the member base** (particularly in cases where Discovery has shown that transactions are happening but there is no connect or feeling for the brand)

How will you achieve this? Every objective has alternative strategic paths or choices. You choose the one best suited to the Organisation's goals and situation. You may choose to reward every transaction made beyond a minimum number. That's a strategy. You may choose to recognise every transaction with a special service benefit. You may choose to have a set of exclusive privileges for the top 5%. You may choose to have a combination of all of the above. Each of the above is a strategic choice.

Typically, you would, at this stage, outline the key strategy elements in your forthcoming design. It may be :

- Program will be inclusive (or exclusive- only for a special few)
- Program will recognize existing loyal customers and give them a headstart
- Tenure of customer will be rewarded
- The family/ household will be the key membership unit (if the brand is relevant to all members of the family)
- Content and communication will be a key driver of behaviour – which will then mean actively driving relevance
- Strong offers to drive behaviour in the mid segments
- Partners will add to the value proposition on offer
- Etc

These are just illustrations. It would depend on the brand, the task, the audience and the key findings of Discovery.

What we have covered are the first two steps of Program Design.

- Prioritise and finalise your objectives. Articulate them well.
- Outline the key strategic elements of your program design.

Then you're good to go for the rest of design.

It's not that hard!

CHAPTER 6

A HOLISTIC PROPOSITION

"The things that make me different are the things that make me, me.." Winnie the Pooh

We're now taking a step forward into the core of Design. The Value Proposition.

What is a Value Proposition?

In the simplest sense it is a statement of purpose. If you can state in one line what you are offering me as a customer, that's your value proposition. It answers the **question "Why should I join your program ?" "Because.......** *(and that's your value proposition!)*

So, how do you arrive at this? And, equally important – how do you articulate it? To yourself and to your customer.

Types of Programs

First, a look at the different types of programs you can have. And remember, these are not watertight compartments. You can have a value proposition that combines multiple offerings because each of these has its pluses and minuses.

- **Points and Rewards Based** – the most common when you say "loyalty program". Essentially the core proposition is that you earn points (or miles or stars – a currency) when you shop, these accrue and you can redeem them for rewards. Rewards may be from a catalogue, it may be against your next shopping, it may be for services – there are various choices.

- **Service Based** – as you shop, you become entitled to services. It could be free parking, it could be free delivery, a shopping assistant, special check-out counter, next-day delivery (Amazon Prime), free returns/replacement etc. Normally, these services are allotted based on slabs of shopping value

- **Discount Based** – There are some programs that are entirely discount based. You become a member and you are entitled to a discount as you shop. Pantaloons Green Card has gone through several avatars, one of them was discount-based. Depending on your tier, you got a % off.

- **Amenities, Recognition, Privilege Based** – The entire proposition could revolve around special recognition and privileges to members. Frequent flyer programs have a component of recognition and privileges as a part of their proposition. You get a special check-in counter, lounge access, priority boarding, priority luggage retrieval etc. Many hotel programs are also strong on special recognition. The room of your choice on priority, upgrade to a suite, a special gift basket placed in the room, customised robes and slippers, a bottle of champagne. The sky is the limit when you're a top tier member.

- **Communication Based** – The entire program rests on relevant communication. So there are largely no offers, services etc – a relationship is built through communication. There are programs that alcohol brands run which are based just on communication. IKEA Family runs strongly on communication interspersed with offers. They use the brand promise of innovation very strongly in their program communication.

- **Partnership Based** – The program bases its offerings on having meaningful and synergistic partners who add value to what the brand is offering its members. So a hotel brand, for e.g., ties up with car rentals, local tourist attractions for its members. Or an apparel retailer with a program ties up with complementary brands as partners – accessories, jewellery, footwear, eye-wear etc.

ARRIVING AT A VALUE PROPOSITION

Arriving at a value proposition is much more than listing the set of offerings that the program will make to its members.

The first step involves deeper introspection into the larger purpose of the program. Yes, it is important to have a larger purpose that goes beyond immediate transactional benefits that the program will deliver to your brand.

A good method is to adopt Simon Sinek's "Start with Why". Simon calls this powerful idea The Golden Circle, and it provides a framework upon which organizations can be built, movements can be led, and people can be inspired. And it all starts with WHY. And it can be used to build your program proposition as well.

SIMON'S GOLDEN CIRCLE

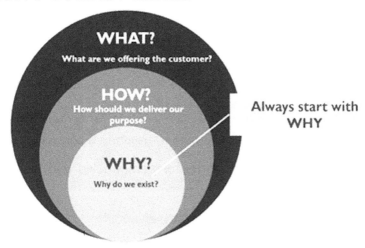

Start with WHY. Why does the program exist (or need to exist)? What is the larger purpose? That will become the true differentiator that stands the test of time.

Once you have articulated the WHY, then you move on to HOW you will achieve this – and finally, WHAT you will therefore offer.

EXAMPLE 1

An Islamic Bank in the Middle East was launching a loyalty program for its customers. The program was rooted in a social cause and **the WHY arrived at was:**

Create and motivate a COMMUNITY of Social Champions who participate consistently and actively by GIVING and DOING such that Social Development for the good of all becomes a self-sustaining and community-driven issue.

The program was introduced to ENERGISE the community to participate in the greater social good.

How did the bank achieve its vision?

- By **creating opportunities** for giving and doing
- By involving the community in the decision making and making it **empowering, democratic and participative**
- By **recognizing and rewarding** participation
- By **being transparent** and sharing information

And, finally, WHAT did the bank offer?

- A multi-dimensional program that rewards and recognizes you for transactional and non-transactional behavior
- A list of causes and institutions empaneled and verified for giving and doing
- Control over your funds disbursal

- Opportunity to enroll others and promote your causes
- Information at your fingertips

The bank could just as easily have started out by saying that they would launch a program that would reward transactions as well as social activities.

By starting out with the WHY, the program had stronger roots, a deeper purpose, a more enduring theme. This helped tie in the whole value proposition in a much stronger fashion.

This does not however mean that a social cause is necessary to define the WHY. We are not looking to force-fit altruism and/or social good in every commercial proposition unless it is there and seamlessly fits in.

EXAMPLE 2

A super-luxury hotel chain was in the process of loyalty program design for its customers. Known for its superior service and exclusivity, the WHY for the program was defined as:

YOU are VALUED by each one of us, every time, everywhere - and we want to make your every stay with us unique, memorable and special

This then translated into the HOW:

- By recognizing who you are and what your preferences are
- By proactively rewarding and appreciating you
- By curating your stay with personalized experiences
- By giving you memories full of surprise and delight

And WHAT was the program then?

A recognition and privileges program that had several exclusive experiences and surprise and delight initiatives that made guests feel exclusive and special with every stay.

When the WHY was articulated as "Valued… every time, everywhere…" "unique, memorable…" the proposition was built on a host of tailormade and customized experiences that would create memories for a lifetime. And this was executed across the chain, at all properties. The program then became more about the experience than the reward though it did have a points and rewards component.

Once you articulate the WHY, HOW and WHAT – and, by the way, this comes after a lot of introspection and intense discussion - you then move on to creating the program architecture.

PROGRAM ARCHITECTURE

The program architecture comprises the **PROGRAM VALUE PROPOSITION** - expressed in a pithy statement, the foundational **DESIGN PRINCIPLES** the program will be based on, and the translation of the value proposition into **PROGRAM PILLARS**.

VALUE PROPOSITION

Use the Golden Circle to express your value proposition in a tightly framed statement.

In our Example 1 above, the Islamic Bank articulated the program Value Proposition as:

By the Community, Of the Community, For the Community

In Example 2, the luxury hotel chain program proposition was:

You will consistently get intuitive, memorable and exclusive experiences from us that recognize how unique, valued and special you are

A fast fashion retailer defined the proposition as:

We will be your ally, your best friend, with you every step of the way - helping you be yourself, helping you realize your potential in the way only you know, and we recognize and reward you through the journey

DESIGN PRINCIPLES

Once the proposition is articulated, get down to design principles that will be the basis of the program. These could be principles like:

- Simplicity and ease

- Choice and control with the member

- Customization

- Multichannel delivery

- Etc

The idea is to articulate the key principles that will underlie everything that you do as part of the program.

PROGRAM PILLARS

A good way to structure your offering is to translate the value proposition into a set of pillars under which you will club program rewards, benefits etc. This helps you remain true to the proposition and instead of a laundry list, you are actually sticking to a set of themes or buckets.

Based on the proposition, the luxury hotel chain defined the program pillars as:

- In-hotel stay experiences
- Exclusive privileges and events
- Partnership offerings

The Islamic Bank defined its pillars as:

- Give for Good - transact, donate

- Do Good – volunteer, participate
- Reap the Good – rewards, benefits, privileges

The fast fashion retailer had three program pillars:

- Content – on fashion and grooming
- Celebrations – rewards and offers
- Community – social networking of like minded

The final step is to depict the Program Architecture in a single graphic. Not critical to do this but immensely helpful as a reference guide when you get down to program rules:

Here are two examples:

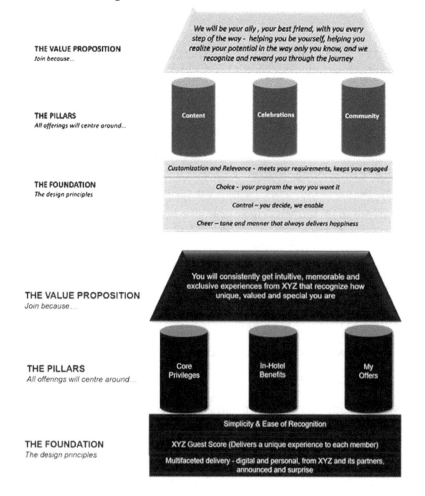

Some useful guidelines to keep in mind when defining the proposition:

1. The most holistic proposition combines HARD BENEFITS and SOFT BENEFITS

   - Hard benefits refer to "economic" and more tangible rewards – points, offers, discounts, sweepstakes etc. They provide RATIONAL value. They are almost hygiene in a program – and remember, they can be easily replicated.

   - Soft Benefits are the softer and more intangible offerings – special service, exclusive access, privileged invitations, more enhanced and seamless shopping experience etc. They provide EMOTIONAL value. Soft benefits are what will truly differentiate your program brand from others. The feel-good value cannot be over-emphasised upon.

2. It is also important to STRETCH PERCEIVED VALUE. When you give a discount or coupon or a gift certificate, the value is transparent and, in the member's mind, is equal to the value offered. A 10% discount is a 10% discount. A 500 INR Gift Certificate will get me something worth 500 INR. When you offer special services (e.g. a Limo drop to the airport for a top tier frequent flyer), the value in the member's mind is far far greater than the cost to the brand. When you enable celebrity access (Meet your hero), no price can be put on the offering. So include a set of exclusive, hard-to-price offerings. The value boost the program will get from these, is immense. Even if only few members actually end up getting these, they will become the talk of the town.

3. DELIVER ASPIRATION – This is similar to stretching perceived value. It also means that you check with your members on their aspirations and include those offerings. Have the "difficult-to-attain" rewards that members will aspire for and accrue their currency. Which means they stick to your brand! Curate rewards that are customized and not available off-the-shelf.

Have a set of experiences that are aspirational – e.g. Redeem your points for an Everest Helicopter Tour in Nepal.

4. HAVE A LARGER CAUSE – While this is not mandatory, it is what will make your program stay the course. Keep in mind the Gen Y, Gen Z and Gen Alpha's mental framework and social consciousness. To resonate with this audience, programs will need to go beyond the transactional. Don't force fit a social cause into the catalogue – like a charity redemption option. Take the effort to link the program to a deeper, larger cause – and it will pay off handsomely in goodwill and stickiness. Members who want to leave the program then will think twice because it means leaving the cause they are affiliated to as well.

Follow these simple guidelines, have a structured approach to value proposition building – and that's the best foundation your program can have.

It's not that hard!

CHAPTER 7

ELIGIBILITY AND MEMBERSHIP

"I refuse to join any club that would have me as a member" Groucho
Marx

We have our objectives and strategy and we have a program proposition. The next step is to decide WHO is eligible for the program, how do we ENROLL them and what are the rules around PROGRAM MEMBERSHIP.

ELIGIBILITY

Who is eligible to become a member of your program, is very closely intertwined with your program objectives and strategy.

Let's say your program objective is to retain and grow your most valuable customers and ring-fence them from leaving. Your strategy may be to create and establish a feeling of exclusivity and recognition that drives usage. The program then becomes available only to your MVCs (Most Valuable Customers) and you will define clear metrics as to what MVC means in terms of value and frequency.

Let's further say that you have secondary objective of driving usage across the board. Your strategy here may be to reward (with offers) mid-value customers to drive their repeat usage. Your program eligibility conditions change. It becomes open to mid-value customers as well but you may then choose to differentiate your MVCs within the program – either through a tier or a program variant.

A brand has no customer level data at all – and is looking at a loyalty program as a way to capture meaningful data. The strategy here may be to enrol everybody because it will result in data capture. Everyone is eligible.

A very high value brand – e.g. a luxury car – will normally choose to have every customer as the program member as well. Every customer is eligible.

So, really, the first decision you are taking on ELIGIBILITY is – IS THE PROGRAM INCLUSIVE OR EXCLUSIVE? OR SOMEWHERE IN BETWEEN? This is a strategic decision that the brand needs to take.

If the program is all-inclusive, then your eligibility criterion may be – anyone who buys (customer) is eligible to be a member. There are also programs where you don't need to "buy" to become a member. Today you can sign up for most hotel programs and airline programs without having stayed a night or taken a flight with the respective brand. Fan clubs essentially comprise "fans" of the brand – whether they have made a transaction or not.

If you do want to have an eligibility criterion, the next step is to set a THRESHOLD that is easy to understand and communicate. Program entry thresholds are most often set based on:

1. Value spent in a specified period (normally 12 months, but it would depend on the category)
2. Frequency of transaction in a specified period
3. A combination of the above - value and/or frequency.

Avoid over-complication with too many eligibility criteria. That makes it difficult to communicate and execute.

Additionally, eligibility can be based on referrals from existing members – a member refers another person, the referee automatically becomes eligible for membership.

The important factor here is that eligibility criteria need to be simple, lucid and transparent. The last is very important. Never have hidden terms and conditions that filter eligibility.

ENROLMENT

How do you enrol members into your program? **Whatever methods you use, whatever processes you follow, ensure they are simple and don't require the customer to jump through hoops**. Keep enrolment flexible whilst ensuring legal compliance.

AUTO OR SOLICITED

Members can be auto-enrolled or solicited for enrolment.

Auto-enrolment implies that you already have a customer database and you AUTOMATICALLY enrol eligible members into your program. Members are sent a welcome message informing them that they are already members. FabIndia did this when they launched FabFamily. Since they had collected mobile numbers of most transacting customers, they launched FabFamily with a ready member base.

Solicited enrolment is where you invite ELIGIBLE customers to become members – and they then ACCEPT membership (or not). This ultimately results in a more involved member base because they chose to enrol consciously into your program.

Auto-enrolment typically results in a larger member base. However, activity levels are likely to be lower – and since members are enrolled automatically, there is no conscious decision making on the part of the member. Awareness and involvement levels are likely to be lower.

Another factor governing enrolment is the prevailing data privacy regulations. Members can be auto-enrolled, but if your program has a currency, members will need to accept program T&Cs before they redeem the currency. This becomes a legal requirement.

CHANNELS OF ENROLMENT

Use multiple channels in tandem so that there is choice. Members choose to enrol via a channel they are most comfortable with. Online enrolment is a must option these days. And social enrolment (through social media channels) is a growing method as well.

Track the channel of enrolment so that you can later identify which has proved the most efficient, the most effective, which gave you the most numbers etc.

ENROLMENT PROCESS

The key to seamless enrolment is simplicity. Typically, the process will involve :

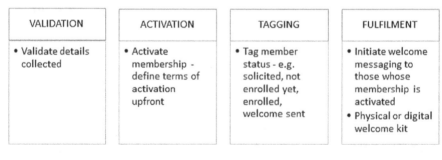

VALIDATION	ACTIVATION	TAGGING	FULFILMENT
• Validate details collected	• Activate membership - define terms of activation upfront	• Tag member status - e.g. solicited, not enrolled yet, enrolled, welcome sent	• Initiate welcome messaging to those whose membership is activated • Physical or digital welcome kit

DATA COLLECTED

Use enrolment as an opportunity to collect customer data – this is especially important if you are building a database from scratch. It is important to categorise data as MANDATORY, NEED TO KNOW AND NICE TO KNOW. This ensures you keep enrolment simple and easy by collecting only mandatory data at the point of enrolment. Use future points of contact to fill in on the "need to know" and "nice to know".

Here is one way of categorising data requirements – though it will vary with the business.

Mandatory	Need to Know	Nice to Know
• Name • Gender • Mobile number	• Email id • Age/DOB • Anniversary • Mailing Address • Family details	• Occupation • Interests and hobbies • Lifestyle/Travel

ENROLMENT - DECISION POINTS

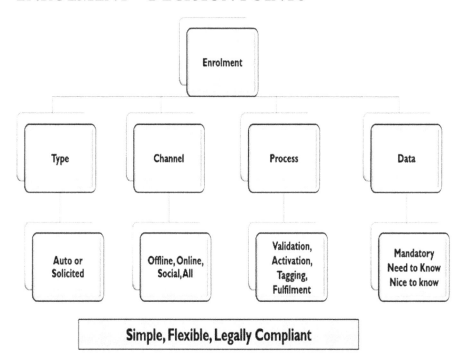

MEMBERSHIP

The first decision point in terms of membership is whether membership is FREE or there will be a FEE charged. This is a strategic decision to be made and heavily linked with the program objectives.

As with all decisions, there are pros and cons to consider.

FREE MEMBERSHIP:

- Suitable when the intent is to have an inclusive program
- Fewer barriers to entry
- Also suitable when it is important to create a base of brand and program "fans" who will spread the word
- Will result in a larger member base, allows for quicker program scaling up and traction
- Lower member expectations and less pressure on delivery
- Activity and commitment levels from members will likely be lower
- Program metrics will show lower impact

MEMBERSHIP FEE:

- Entry barrier, will result in a smaller but more committed member base
- Higher member involvement and investment in the program
- Improved metrics, also because of a self-selection bias – high value customers will find it more beneficial and relevant to pay the fee
- Member expectations and demands will be higher – pressure to deliver the committed value proposition on the ground consistently
- Will ultimately likely result in a more differentiated program

Membership fee charged by programs is often offset by immediate delivery of value to the member that makes the equation appear attractive – e.g. points of same (or higher) value credited to the member account as a welcome bonus, brand coupons or partner offers worth much more than the membership fee or a special welcome gift hamper.

Some programs have a hybrid option of free and paid membership – the paid membership is for an elevated set of benefits. Shoppers Stop First Citizen Black is a paid program - a membership fee of INR 4500 per year entitles the member to a premium offering. The base First Citizen program has a much lower membership fee of INR 350. It was initially a free program subject to minimum purchase - they have since introduced a membership fee for that as well.

IKEA Family is a free program – and does not even have an eligibility condition of purchase. You can become a member of IKEA Family and follow all of their news and product offerings via program communication. Very good way to build up a set of devoted IKEA fans even if they don't shop at IKEA just yet!!

LuluLemon – the Athleisure and sportswear brand from Canada – has free and paid program variants – Essential and Studio. The Studio variant involves the purchase of a Studio Mirror and then entitles the member to a set of workout regimes and classes – apart from other elevated benefits.

Payback India, now rebranded as Zillion – is a free program. One can join the program online and then shop at any of the coalition brands later.

It is important to keep in mind that PAID MEMBERSHIP is slightly different from a PAID PRODUCT OR SERVICE OFFERING. Amazon Prime is Paid Membership that entitles you to an elevated offering that includes content and services - for a membership period of one year (or one month or three months – depending on the term signed up for). When you choose to fly Business or First Class on an airline, you are PAYING for the elevated privileges that you get for that ONE TIME that you fly. The next time, you have to BUY the offering again. The same is true for stays in Suites and Premium rooms in hotels.

OTHER MEMBERSHIP DECISIONS

Once a decision has been taken on FREE vs FEE, the next set of decision points include:

1. MEMBERSHIP ENTITY – Is the membership entity the individual, the household, the business unit? For most consumer programs the individual is the membership entity. When the brand is relevant to the entire household, the membership "entity" may rest with the household. And for B2B programs, a decision needs to be taken on whether the entity is the entire business or the SBU or the Branch etc.

2. POINT OF CONTACT – Who is the point of contact for all program communication? For individual programs, the entity and the point of contact are the same. When it comes to Household programs, there is typically a PRIMARY MEMBER who is the main point of contact and ADD-ON or ASSOCIATE MEMBERS who may receive specific communication. Programs will need to limit the maximum number of add-on or associate members allowed, for greater standardisation and control. For B2B programs, it is important to identify the DECISION MAKING UNIT (DMU), define primary and associate members within this and then segment communication appropriately. Typically there is a USER, INFLUENCER AND DECISION MAKER in the DMU (e.g. Admin, HR and CxO) and each would be targeted with different messaging

3. HOUSEHOLDING – Programs which allow Primary and Associate membership need to decide whether they will allow HOUSEHOLDING or not. **Householding is when all currency earned by all the members of the household is pooled into a central household account.** This allows for greater cumulative

velocity of earning. As a corollary there would then be rules on who is allowed to redeem those points. For greater control, redemption is often centred with the Primary Member only.

4. IDENTIFIER – In today's programs, the membership identifier is most often the mobile number. This is the simplest and most customer friendly option. Members are asked for their mobile numbers when they shop and the system can track their history. The loyalty system will allot a UNIQUE MEMBERSHIP NUMBER to each member at the back-end - however, no member is expected to remember this. In the case of Householding, the system will allot a HOUSEHOLD ID at the back-end and then link individual membership ids to a single household id.

5. CARDING – Physical carding is almost non-existent today given the administrative hassles involved in sending out the cards – and the costs. More so, because people hardly carry around their cards these days. Digital carding - often embedded into program mobile apps – is the way to go. As one example, the entire Starbucks rewards program works off the app. There are however exceptional cases where carding is still relevant – and especially so in India. Smaller towns in India, where loyalty programs are still gaining presence, still value physical cards as a sign of esteem and prestige. Channel programs (for dealers, distributors etc) may also choose to have physical cards as devices that demonstrate respect and esteem. Super premium programs for really exclusive audiences sometimes also choose to go with exclusively designed physical cards. When the program membership card is a co-branded credit card, then physical carding is a must. Saks First, the membership program of Saks Fifth Avenue, is co-branded with Mastercard.

6. VALIDITY – Important to define validity of membership. There are different options – it could be "lifetime" as long as the member is "active" – and activity levels then need to be

defined clearly. Membership validity could also be yearly, multiples of years. The critical point is to define it and not leave it open-ended.

A NOTE ON HOUSEHOLDING

Householding makes immense sense in the following scenarios:

- The brand is relevant to the entire family and has a product and service range that works across ages and genders
- The brand is relevant to the "household" as a unit – e.g. Grocery and department store brands, banking and financial services
- Where experiences can be served to the family as a unit – travel and hospitality
- Household is not just the "family" but also "affinity groups" where the social shopping factor is common – entertainment, QSRs, fan clubs, fashion and accessories

RENEWAL

Linked to membership validity are the terms for membership renewal. In order to ensure legal compliance – and also to separate the wheat from the chaff (improve program metrics and activity levels) – membership renewals are an important process to follow. Members who are less involved, inactive, low users etc will tend not to renew and this ultimately improves the overall health of the member base.

There could be auto- renewal of membership for active members - and this will be built into the program T&Cs. This reduces process and administrative hassles to a great extent.

Renewal terms may be set to easier thresholds than eligibility terms so as to minimise extreme leakage of membership - so if there is a value or transaction threshold to become eligible for membership, once you become a member you can retain membership if you achieve at least 75-80% of that threshold in a pre-specified period (normally one year).

A good way to drive renewals is to have offers – make sure the offers are relevant and meaningful. Not a blind set of brand vouchers that most satellite TV operators seem to offer these days for renewal of packages! Also, make sure that choice of offers is limited – a plethora of offers leads to confusion and paralysis of action.

The key principles to follow to define eligibility, drive enrolment, set membership rules and motivate renewals are:

- Keep it simple
- Ensure transparency and clarity
- Always keep objectives in mind

It's not that hard!

CHAPTER 8

CURRENCY PRINCIPLES

"Could you spare a small smackerel?" — *Winnie the Pooh*

Often the core of the value proposition. Program Currency. Call it points, miles, stars, coins – or innovative names like Smiles, Credits, Wows, (Smackerel??!) – what have you.

Before we delve deeper into this - No – it is not mandatory for a program to have a currency. We have dealt with different types of loyalty programs earlier – and you can have a strong differentiated proposition without a currency. IKEA Family does not have a currency. It has a strong enough proposition centred around special prices, curated solutions and innovative communication.

However, when you think "loyalty program" – the top-of-mind reaction is most often "Points and Rewards". Currency is an integral part of most program propositions. It is, undeniably, the tangible hard benefit that is easiest to recall and vocalise.

It is important to define a sustainable currency strategy and structure the program earn such that it is ATTRACTIVE to the member and AFFORDABLE to the brand.

Let us explore three areas with reference to currency:

1. Where does a currency work best?
2. What should the earn criteria be?
3. How do you structure the currency table?

WHERE DOES A CURRENCY WORK BEST?

Program currency is like a ticker. It needs to tick regularly, consistently – and meaningfully. Only then is it relevant to the member. ABSOLUTE EARN and VELOCITY OF EARN are both critical factors that tell you whether a currency makes sense for your program.

ABSOLUTE EARN

How much can your program afford to give back as currency? Is it substantial enough such that the member can get a reasonable reward within 3-6 months of membership?

There are two ways to take a decision on ABSOLUTE EARN – also called ABSOLUTE GIVEBACK. The brand may take a decision to INVEST in the loyalty program and arrives at what is believed to be an affordable giveback. The other way is to take a % of margin and allocate it to points giveback - normally this is funded by the marketing budget or through sales/distribution margins. No ballpark numbers here – it will vary widely by business and it's not advisable to generalise.

As a very general benchmark however, grocery is a very low margin category – giveback in points would not be more that 0.5%- 1% of sale value. The same is true for telecom. Fuel as a category is notoriously low margin and will not be able to afford more than 0.1% - 0.3% as giveback. Apparel and accessories would be anywhere between 3-5%. Travel and hospitality would also be in the 3-5% range. High margin categories (jewellery, appliances, F&B) can go upto 10% in giveback. E-commerce players offer anywhere between 2-4%.

To drive up absolute earn, grocery players will tend to reward differentially by category - private label products (which have a higher margin) will give more currency earn than branded products for e.g. Fuel players, similarly, offer higher givebacks on lubricants, convenience stores and services to beef up the earn levels.

So the first step is to evaluate how much you can give back and will it be viewed as motivating by the member.

VELOCITY OF EARN

How fast can the currency be earned? Are there reasonably frequent interactions that allow for accrual of earn? In the case of grocery for example, while the absolute giveback may be 1% or less, there is a weekly frequency that keeps the ticker going. In the case of telecom, the frequency of usage is daily (hourly). Fuel frequency may be weekly or fortnightly.

Apparel and accessories, department stores will have 3-6 monthly frequency – so the velocity is lower. For a frequent traveller, velocity of earn is high for both airline and hotel programs. That's the reason why these programs consciously target the business traveller.

In the case of a high value purchase – real estate, automobiles, durables/appliances – the absolute earn as a % of purchase value may result in a substantial sum. But there is no frequency of interaction thereafter to keep the counter ticking. Automobile programs therefore will actively drive frequency through incentivisation of additional interactions. Servicing, repairs, spares, accessories, referrals, usage of support services - all these will help increase the frequency of interaction and help improve velocity. Real estate thrives on referrals as a reward earning behaviour.

A currency therefore works best when both absolute earn and velocity of earn are high. It is important that at least one of these factors is present to justify currency in a program.

Let's look at a very broad characterisation of businesses by Margin and Velocity of Earn.

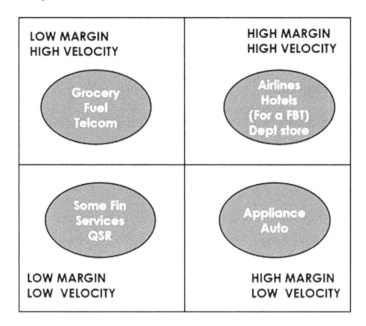

While these are some examples, it depends heavily on the "affordable" giveback as described earlier. Some businesses may consciously choose to invest in loyalty in the early years and therefore give back more than their margins would perhaps allow through alternate sources of funding.

WHAT SHOULD THE EARN CRITERIA BE?

For what behaviour will the member earn the currency?

Choose the key business metric that the program needs to drive, as the basis for currency earn. Across most businesses this will be VALUE of purchase. So a % of sale value is given back as points.

There are businesses that expect the program to help drive frequency of usage. So members will then earn points for NUMBER of transactions done, irrespective of value. In the early days of e-commerce, the need was to cultivate the online shopping habit. Frequency was the key metric for most players.

For some products – especially B2B, industrial – VOLUME or TONNAGE – may be the key business metric. As an example, cement is sold in tonnes - since pricing is regulated, tonnage is the key metric.

The founding principle is to integrate earn strongly with the key business metric so that the program feeds into the organisation objectives seamlessly.

It is important to note however that earn criteria must be **multi-dimensional and holistic.** The members then find the program exciting and more rewarding. It is therefore critical to reward OTHER DESIRABLE BEHAVIOUR – transactional and non-transactional.

Transactional behaviour beyond the key metric may be – a new product trial, a pack size, an SKU, private label purchase, other special business goals that need to be incentivised.

Non-transactional behaviour could be – filling up profile information, visiting the website, logging on to the app, playing a game, filling a survey, giving feedback, goodwill earn for special occasions like a birthday, anniversary or festival etc.

Which brings us to the next question of how to structure earn such that it is holistic and yet within the allowable.

STRUCTURING THE EARN TABLE

This is an iterative process and deeply integrated with the financial modelling for the loyalty program which we will delve into in a later chapter. But let's look at first principles for structuring earn.

Here is one logical way :

- Start with a TOTAL ALLOWABLE EARN – this is based on margin or an affordable earn given that the brand is investing in loyalty. Let's say this figure is 7%.

- Divide this TOTAL EARN into BASE EARN and BONUS EARN.

- BASE EARN is what it says – the absolute base earn for business-as-usual, rewarded for the key business metric (whether value or volume or tonnage or frequency)

- BONUS EARN is what you allocate for OTHER DESIRABLE BEHAVIOUR that you need the program to drive. This may be any of the transactional or non-transactional behaviour specified above. BONUS EARN is further divided into

  - ONGOING BONUS - e.g. you may choose to reward Private Label purchase throughout the year; or **value** is your base earn metric but **frequency** is an ongoing bonus.

  - TACTICAL BONUS – this is a kitty kept aside that is used tactically for short-term behaviour drives – e.g. a referral campaign, a feedback campaign, a particular new product trial, a new payment method etc. The brand may introduce new earn criteria every quarter and award bonus currency - this keeps the program novel and flexible

  - RELATIONSHIP BONUS – or GOODWILL bonus issued for special occasions and milestones – e.g. birthdays, anniversaries, festivals. More importantly, a WELCOME BONUS that kicks off the accrual and steps up member motivation.

Bonus earn is also sometimes categorised as:

- Spatial – Bonus for transacting via a particular channel, at a particular place/outlet

- Temporal – Bonus related to time – like a happy hour bonus, weekday vs weekend, on enrolment, festival bonus

- Transactional – purely related to the transaction – a specific SKU bought, a payment instrument used

- Personal – for personal milestones and goodwill – birthdays, anniversaries, attaining a tier, completing one year of membership etc

The thumb-rule to follow in terms of the base:bonus split is:

- When you launch a program, keep the base:bonus ratio at about 70:30 because you want members to get into the program habit and earn for behaviour that they were doing anyway. So for a 7% total allowable, you would allocate approx. 5% to base earn and the balance to bonus earn.

- As the program evolves you will slowly move towards a 50:50 ratio; a mature program may in fact have a 30:70 skew towards bonus because the goal is to drive more and more new behaviour.

- Also, remember that the allowable figure will also increase as the program starts delivering returns. So from a 7% launch earn figure you may start moving up to 8-10% in a couple of years. It becomes very critical to deploy the earn effectively such that it drives incremental program revenue.

Another factor to keep in mind while structuring earn is how to structure BASE EARN. Let's say value is the key metric to incentivise. There are different ways to structure the earn:

1. Arithmetic Progression – it is a % of total bill value – and improves arithmetically as bill value increases. This rewards value but does not actively motivate higher spends

2. Geometric Progression - % of total bill value upto a threshold, thereafter it scales to a higher % value till the next threshold - and so on. This actively drives higher purchase value. You are also consciously rewarding high performers more than proportionately.

3. Fixed Earn Slabs – E.g. A spend of INR 101- 300 earns 20 points, 301-500 earns 50 points etc. This does not differentiate member

spends within the slab and helps keep costs under control but doesn't really reward incremental behaviour.

There may be other options as well – the trick is to make it innovative as well as efficient and effective. And, most of all, easy to communicate.

CURRENCY VALIDITY AND EXPIRY

This is a critical rule to keep in mind when you have a program currency. Currency must expire. You cannot have it lasting endlessly because the liability in your books will balloon uncontrollably.

Not only must you have a validity/expiry rule, it must also be communicated with clarity.

When a program currency is issued, it is not a cash outflow in your loyalty accounts – it is a deferred liability that has to be paid against future sale recorded.

When you set a validity for your currency, keep in mind the following:

1. Your "average" member should be able to accumulate enough to redeem a reasonable reward before the currency expires

2. Your "best" member should be able to accumulate enough for your larger and more aspirational rewards

SETTING VALIDITY RULES

Validity rules are normally set based on MONTH OF EARN to keep it simple and systematic.

Ideally you would allow validity for a 24-months to 36-months period (from month of earn) so that there is sufficient accrual. Post this set period, the currency expires and the value accounted for is added back into the books straight to the bottom line.

Some programs allow only a 12-month validity. Where there is high frequency of transaction, and hence high velocity of earn (e.g. Grocery, telecom) this is possible because there is likely to be sufficient accrual even in a 12 month period.

When the currency is about to expire, as a best practice, enough forewarning needs to be given to the member to redeem the same before expiry.

Validity of currency is also linked to member activity in the program. If membership expires, unredeemed currency of the member would also expire immediately regardless of any remaining currency validity.

BRANDING OF CURRENCY

Too little importance is given to what is really a huge branding opportunity and can leverage the program and the brand in more ways than one.

The moment you have a currency in your program, it is an opportunity for branding and recall - to become part of the program lingo.

It is the easiest thing in the world to have an addendum to the program brand name - XYZ Points/Miles/Stars/Rewards – and that is your currency brand. However, a little effort put into this will pay off in spades. Yes, it must have the program brand as part of the name but add a bit of creativity so that the currency itself stands for something.

Payback India has recently re-branded itself as Zillion – and the currency is also Zillion Coins. The goal is to make the program ubiquitous across categories – so that the member can literally earn a Zillion coins for everyday spends. Good branding!

Nordstrom's The Nordy Club has the concept of NORDSTROM NOTES – where points are converted into fixed value NORDSTROM NOTES which can be used against purchase.

There is no need to over-complicate or give esoteric names. But a little innovation and creative thinking goes a long way in adding to the brand equity.

To round off, the fundamental principles to follow in your currency strategy :

1. Keep it simple - the member should be able to calculate – and understand.

2. Ensure it is multidimensional and flexible

3. Be Innovative in structuring your earn table

4. Be Clear in your communication.

5. Stick to your budgeted value

6. Set an expiry for the currency

It's not that hard.

CHAPTER 9

TIERING STRATEGY AND PRINCIPLES

"I always said Tiggers could climb trees. Not that it's easy, mind you. Of course, there's the coming-down too. Which will be difficult unless one fell, when it would be easy."
— *Tigger, Winnie the Pooh*

The member base in a program needs to aspire to climb higher, to get more. That's when the program is motivating and stickiness improves. And that is where tiers come in.

There is a view that says - TIERING IS HISTORY. "Segment of One" is the way to go. Technology today enables that – we can actually address each customer/member individually and drive relevance, so why have tiers. You are able to motivate each member (segment of one remember!) individually and change behaviour. True – but covert.

Tiers are the most basic segmentation. They are an **external manifestation** of program aspiration and do wonders for social esteem and for the feeling of exclusivity and privilege that program membership brings.

SHOULD YOU ALWAYS HAVE TIERS IN A PROGRAM?

This does not mean, however, that tiers are warranted in every program. It is program data that will tell you if there is sufficient disparity between member segments to warrant differentiated propositions. You perhaps find that there is the top 5% of your member base giving you close to 30% of revenue from the total member base. Surely this warrants that they are ring-fenced more than others because a loss of even one member from this group will impact revenue significantly.

When there are distinct transaction segments emerging, tiers are warranted. Remember that you will look at transaction data from the lens of the key metric you are driving through the program. If you are driving revenue, look at transaction data in terms of revenue per customer/ member. If you are driving frequency then look at average frequency per member.

In categories like grocery, fashion, department store, specialty retail etc, where customer-level transaction data is not normally available, the loyalty program is the tool to enrol members and capture this data. In such cases you would normally launch the program with no tiers because you don't have an idea yet as to how members are behaving. Where customer-level transaction data is available in the system (telecom, hotels, airlines, e-commerce etc), you may choose to analyse previous 12 months data when you launch the program, decide on a tier structure if relevant – and directly enrol members into tiers they qualify for. In this case you launch the program with tiers.

When taking a decision on whether to have tiers or not, it is good to ask yourself, first and foremost, whether you can deliver sufficiently differentiated tier propositions on the ground. If that's not a clear "yes", don't have tiers. If members belong to different tiers, they must be treated differently. And in tangible, meaningful ways. Always wise not to have tiers just for the sake of having them.

Tiering strategy will involve taking a decision across several crucial areas:

1. Tier criteria
2. No. of tiers
3. Tier thresholds - for attainment and retention
4. Tier upgrade and downgrade rules
5. Tier-wise differentiated proposition
6. Branding of tiers

TIER CRITERIA

Yes your program needs tiers as per data analysis. What should tiers be based on?

Always use the key business metric as the guideline. If it is value, tiers should be set based on value. If frequency, then frequency slabs will define tiers.

Sometimes you can have tiers with two criteria – and it can be an AND or OR condition. E.g. Value and Frequency.

- You can define the base tier for eligibility as TWO TRANSACTIONS OR INR 1000 in value. Either condition satisfies eligibility criteria for the program

- It can also be TWO TRANSACTIONS AND INR 1000 in value. Both conditions have to be satisfied for eligibility. One transaction of INR 1000+ will not do. And two transactions of INR 250 each will not do either

Having multiple criteria, however, is always more complicated to communicate internally to frontline staff and to customers as well. Unless the two metrics are equally critical, avoid using multiple criteria to define tiers.

KEEP IT SIMPLE, EASY TO COMMUNICATE, EASY TO CALCULATE. Members themselves should, at a pinch, be able to arrive at which tier they belong to and what they need to do in order to upgrade to the next tier.

NO. OF TIERS

There are no hard and fast rules on the right number of tiers to have. There are two ways to go about this:

- First, look at your transaction data (based on the key metric) and see where the natural breaks in the data distribution occur. This will tell you how many broad segments you are looking at

- Second, take a hard look at the loyalty readiness within the organisation and evaluate how capable you are to deliver differentiated propositions on the ground and as a tangible offering to the segments. Only if they are sufficiently differentiated will you be able to drive movement upwards.

Based on this, you will arrive at a targeted number of tiers. As a very broad thumb rule, when a program launches tiers, it would not be wise to go with more than three at the start. Try and create three value propositions, each more elevated than the previous and you will realise how difficult it is. More than three is tough to manage at the start.

The priority is really your top 5-10% of customers and creating a carefully crafted, truly exclusive and differentiated proposition for them. As a first step in tiering, you may choose to have just the premium tier and the rest of the member base.

While it is not advisable to change the program structure too frequently (it portrays indecision and instability in the program), it is equally necessary to evaluate the program structure every two years to check for stability and movement. This will indicate whether the structure needs to be tweaked to add tiers at the top, middle or bottom.

Most often programs will find after about two years of launching tiers that either

1. The base tier is swelling AND/OR

2. The top tier has become unmanageable

This is because more and more members are entering the program at the base (a good thing!) or more and more are qualifying for the top tier and the program performance as a whole is improving (also a good thing!).

This will warrant a re-look at thresholds and an introduction of either a super-premium tier at the top or an additional tier at the bottom. The iconic erstwhile Jet Privilege program (now Intermiles) had launched with Blue, Silver and Gold tiers. Later they introduced a Blue Plus (above Blue but below Silver) and a Platinum (above Gold) tier.

When Titan Industries integrated all its individual brand programs into Titan Encircle, they launched with three tiers – Silver, Gold and Platinum. They continue with the same structure today even after close to a decade.

Marriott Bonvoy progressively introduced tiers at the top - Beyond Silver/Gold/Platinum Elite, we have Titanium Elite and Ambassador Elite.

THE ANSWER LIES IN THE DATA. Look at it carefully and judiciously – tempered with pragmatism.

TIER THRESHOLDS

We have already discussed tier criteria and the use of the key business metric/s to set thresholds.

Once you have finalised the number of tiers your program will have, the next step is to actually fix the thresholds. Peg the number (value or frequency or any other metric) at which the next tier starts.

There are simple steps to follow whilst setting thresholds:

1. First look at the AVERAGE METRICS (in a specified period – e.g. a year) across the segments (prospective tiers) you have divided your member base into. Let's say there are three tiers and the average revenue **per member** in Tier 1 is 10,000 INR p.a., in Tier 2 it is 45,000 INR and in Tier 3 it is 1,50,000 INR

2. Next, look at the SPREAD of the same metric in each tier. So for Tier 1 the range of revenue is from 100 INR (min) to 20,000 INR (max). For Tier 2 it is 25,000 INR (min) to 75,000 INR (max). For Tier 3 it is 80,000 INR (min) to 450,000 INR (max).

3. Third, look at what % of the base in each tier is centred around the Average (+/- 15%).

4. Fourth look at what % of the base in the Lower and Middle tiers are about 90% of the Min of the tier that is just higher. So, what % of the base in the Lowest tier is within 90% of 25,000 INR and what % of the base in the middle tier is within 90% of INR 80,000

These 4 sets of numbers will give you direction to set thresholds that are achievable with a stretch – yet not so unattainable that the whole tier structure is demotivating and looked at with scepticism. You want to push the metrics higher but want people to be able to upgrade as well.

So you may then set thresholds like – Upto 25,000 INR p.a. per member is the base tier. From 25,001 INR to 100,000 INR is the middle tier and >100,000 INR is the top tier.

As a thumb rule set thresholds as **round (whole) numbers** around the desired figure, that are easy to remember. A threshold set as 24,750 INR for e.g. is a needless complication!

Another added tactic is to set **different thresholds for ATTAINMENT of a tier and RETENTION** of the tier. So, in the above example, a member needs to purchase worth 25,000 INR p.a. to attain the middle tier. But once he attains the tier, he can retain it as long as he spends 20,000 INR in a 12-month period from attainment. Why is this done? To prevent excessive downgrades which can upset the program structure apart from being deeply demotivating to the member.

TIER UPGRADE AND DOWNGRADE RULES

It is important to clearly specify upgrade and downgrade rules if your program has tiers. There should be no ambiguity and the communication on upgrades, potential downgrades and downgrades needs to be lucid and timely.

Most programs follow a simple principle. Upgrades are given the moment a member reaches the threshold of the tier above. This drives up motivation and aspiration. So a member is in the Base Tier from January. By April (4 months) he has achieved the threshold for the Mid Tier. He will be upgraded to the Mid Tier in May.

Downgrades are evaluated in a 12-month period. So, once a member attains a tier, he/she can retain the tier and get the tier benefits for a minimum of 12 months from date of attainment, regardless of performance.

Downgrade rules can also differ by tier. So for a super-premium tier (your top 1%), you may choose to have a longer tier validity (e.g. 2 years, 5 years) or even lifetime membership of the tier. This is a business call that needs to be taken after evaluating the financial impact of such a decision.

Tier upgrades and downgrades are very important communication nudges. "Fence-sitter" campaigns are sent to members who are just below the upper tier threshold, urging them to attain the same to reap elevated benefits. Congratulatory messages on upgrading are a standard practice.

Downgrades are potentially sensitive and cause member angst – and some programs choose not to downgrade members at all, to avoid potential discontent. This is bad practice. Downgrades are a must to keep the program structure stable and motivating. What is important is to handle the downgrades professionally and with empathy. Give plenty of notice before a downgrade. Have offers and deals that will drive behaviour that avoids the downgrades. Just before a downgrade, make sure communication goes out informing the member she is about to be downgraded.

The tone and manner of downgrade communication is important. Too often it is treated as a statutory notification with officious language, when it is actually an opportunity to drive behaviour and reinforce program benefits.

Think of the difference between:

"You have spent only xxx in the last 12 months and as per program rules you will be downgraded to Silver from May 1st"

Vs

"We notice that you have spent xxx since last May. As a result you would qualify for the Silver tier from next month. We look forward to welcoming you back at the store this month. By just spending yyy, you will be able to retain your Gold tier and continue to enjoy benefits such as……"

TIER-WISE DIFFERENTIATED PROPOSITIONS

This is the most critical part of a program's tiering strategy. What elevated propositions are you going to give your members as they upgrade such that they remain motivated and active in the program?

The moment a program has overt and published tiers, it is very important that the perceived difference between tiers is tangible. Equally important that members are able to vocalise what they will receive on upgrading. *"If I become a Platinum member, this is what I will get additionally…."* *"Platinum members get 6 complimentary airport lounge visits "*

While it is basic hygiene that the earn rate improves for higher tiers, what differentiates a good program is that the component of softer and more and more curated benefits, privileges and recognition keeps going up as tiers improve. So too the opportunities for physical events and face-to-face interaction - since the numbers in the top tiers are more manageable, events are easier to pull off. Communication becomes more and more tailor-made, fine-tuned and relevancy improves by leaps and bounds.

Here is a typical tier-wise differentiated proposition structure:

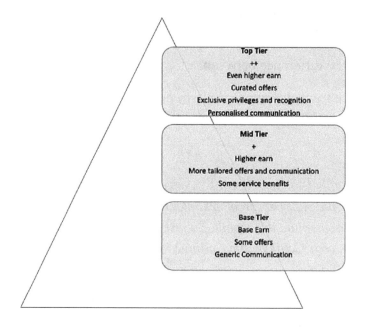

It is important to remember that for every tier, the proposition offered must reflect the overall program purpose and goal. And ensure that you have the bandwidth and the wherewithal for more and more curation and customisation for the top tiers – whether it is in communication, in rewards, in benefits, in privileges or in customer service.

All program literature that is published to members must be able to **visually connote** elevated tier propositions. The basic principle that tiers must drive aspiration needs to be translated into all communication with respect to tiering. So instead of program literature conveying benefits tier by tier, a single snapshot showing the elevation in proposition is much more impactful.

Here are some examples:

HARRODS REWARDS

Green: up to £1,999	Green 2: £2,000-£4,999	Gold: £5,000-£9,999	Black: £10,000+
• 1 point earned for every £1 spent • Exclusive discount days • Extra Rewards points on specially selected days • Invitation to Mini Harrods	• 1 point earned for every £1 spent • Exclusive discount days • Extra Rewards points on specially selected days • Invitation to join Mini Harrods • Complimentary Harrods Magazine • Complimentary Gift Wrapping • Complimentary UK standard delivery when shopping in-store over £250 • Complimentary tea or coffee in-store	• 2 points earned for every £1 spent • Exclusive discount days • Extra Rewards points on specially selected days • Invitation to join Mini Harrods • Complimentary Harrods Magazine • Complimentary Gift Wrapping • Complimentary UK standard delivery when shopping in-store • Complimentary tea or coffee in-store • Two extra 10% discount days per year • Eligibility to apply for the exclusive Harrods American Express® card • Complimentary basic alterations with The Tailors	• 3 points earned for every £1 spent • Exclusive discount days • Extra Rewards points on specially selected days • Invitation to join Mini Harrods • Complimentary Harrods Magazine • Complimentary Gift Wrapping • Complimentary UK standard delivery when shopping in-store • Complimentary tea or coffee in-store • Two extra 10% discount days per year • Eligibility to apply for the exclusive Harrods American Express® card • Complimentary basic alterations with The Tailors • Two hours' complimentary car parking at Harrods Brompton Place

NEIMAN MARCUS INCIRCLE

BENEFIT + ANNUAL SPEND LEVEL	CIRCLE ONE ($1+)	CIRCLE TWO ($1,000+)	CIRCLE THREE ($2,500+)	CIRCLE FOUR ($5,000+)	CIRCLE FIVE ($10,000+)
INCIRCLE CONCIERGE*				■	■
FREE GIFT PACKAGING* in stores and online			■	■	■
PERK CARD*			$25 PERK CARD		ADDITIONAL $50 PERK CARD
DOUBLE POINT DAY*		■	■	■	■
FREE 2-DAY SHIPPING online · catalog orders		■	■	■	■
BONUS-POINT EVENTS*		■	■	■	■

BRANDING OF TIERS

And, finally, a pet peeve. Branding of tiers. It is simplest and easiest to communicate when you say – Blue, Silver, Gold, Platinum. The member is also clear which are the higher tiers.

So, if there's a crunch or nothing else really fits, by all means, go ahead with Silver, Gold, Platinum. It is simple, it is lucid.

Some programs have made a conscious attempt to brand their tiers in tune with the brand personality. **Gap Good Rewards has three tiers – Core, Enthusiast and Icon.**

Sephora Beauty Insider – a hallmark program – has branded its tiers : Insider, VIB (Very Important Beauty Insider) and Rouge. Not easy to identify which is the higher tier between VIB and Rouge, but very representative of the brand.

Closer home, **Levi's Loop has Indigo (reflective of blue jeans), Copper and Gold** as the program tiers. **Raymond's My Raymond program has Prestige, Privilege and Signature.**

Shoppers Stop First Citizen has Silver Edge, Golden Glow, Platinum Aura and Black. The simple addition of a word to the "Silver, Gold and Platinum" has elevated the branding.

Look at tiers as an additional branding opportunity and leverage the same.

Finally, rounding off with some quick tips:

1. Evaluate whether your program needs tiers or not. Use data

2. Proceed step by step to ensure differentiated delivery on the ground

3. Evaluate tier performance year on year – check for upgrades and downgrades – to see whether the program structure needs to be tweaked.

Yes, it's simple. Not that hard!

CHAPTER 10

REWARDS AND REDEMPTION

"You might just as well say," added the March Hare, "that 'I like what I get' is the same thing as 'I get what I like'!" Alice in *Wonderland*

Time to take a pause and do a recap on what we have covered so far.

The Loyalty Program design process started with a detailed DISCOVERY exercise.

Having set the guardrails and framework for the program, we then moved into PROGRAM DESIGN.

- We learnt how to PRIORITISE and LAYER OBJECTIVES
- We defined the KEY STRATEGIC ELEMENTS for the program
- We went into designing a HOLISTIC VALUE PROPOSITION and the reason WHY
- We then converted the value proposition into the PROGRAM ARCHITECTURE with PILLARS and ground rules
- Moving on, we looked into ELIGIBILITY CRITERIA and the options available

- We went into ENROLMENT PROCESS and requisite DATA CAPTURE
- We covered the principles of MEMBERSHIP and RENEWAL
- We defined the CURRENCY STRATEGY and rules around program currency
- And we went into the decisions on TIERING and defining TIER-WISE PROPOSITIONS

And now, we have come to what is, arguably, the biggest moment of truth in the program. Rewards and Redemption.

Let us first understand two concepts:

1. REDEMPTION – Redemption is when the member uses the currency earned in the program to get a gift or reward. S/ He will either use the points/miles during the next purchase, adjusted against the bill at the stated value per unit of currency – or can use the same to get items from a catalogue designed for this purpose. When currency is redeemed it is deducted from the member's account and accounted for in the sale (or catalogue redemption).

2. BREAKAGE – When currency is not redeemed, it expires at the end of the validity period. This expired value is then written back into the books as profit and this is known as breakage. So, let's say a member has 1000 points. 800 are redeemed. Thereafter, the member becomes less active or finds nothing worthwhile to redeem for. Hence 200 points expire at the end of 24 months (the validity period set). This 200 points is your breakage. And it is written back into the books at the accounted value of the points. So if 1 point = INR 1, INR 200 is the breakage value.

There are some basic REDEMPTION BEST PRACTICES to keep in mind:

1. Always design for redemption. You want members to redeem. You want them to experience the biggest moment of truth. Good programs actively encourage redemption to drive home this value.

2. As a corollary to this, don't design for breakage. Don't financially forecast program viability assuming high breakage. This looks good on paper but detracts from the program value – and ultimately the program suffers. Many credit card programs suffer from this design flaw. They ASSUME low redemption and high breakage in their financial model. So they account for 100 million points issued but then forecast a 20% redemption and potentially 80 million profit write-back. This is self-defeating!

3. Communicate on redemption – ACTIVELY, IN TIME and RELEVANTLY. All three matter.

   • Remind members to redeem their points. There should a fair quota of "redemption communication" in your communication plan

   • When points have accumulated sufficiently for a first reward, remind them. When points are about to expire, remind them. Always communicate that you want members to redeem. You're not here to issue points and then let them expire for your benefit.

   • Drive relevance – based on the member's transaction history and profile information you can actually cue rewards that will be relevant to the member.

4. Have drives that help you wipe out liability – Redemption at half the required points, specially curated items for redemption, sale items for redemption – these campaigns get more and more members redeeming and this helps wipe out liability

from your books. And since redemption transactions almost invariably result in a revenue bump, there is tangible financial benefit to the program as well.

5. Drive high perceived value through your redemption catalogue. Curation, relevance, customisation – all drive higher value.

A good redemption rate is when you have 40-50% of your MEMBERS redeeming and about 50-60% of points being redeemed.

PRINCIPLES FOR DESIGNING A GOOD REDEMPTION CATALOGUE

Time was when redemption catalogues used to be designed annually and there were "windows" open for redemption. Catalogues were physical – and there was little flexibility to add or delete items once finalised. Not so any more. Catalogues are dynamic and redemption is ongoing for most programs. Channel programs however may still have redemption windows (often half-yearly) for simplicity of execution.

- The simplest way to drive redemption is to allow for redemption for own products seamlessly during a sale transaction. Most retail programs follow this. It drives greater redemption, more members redeeming and is also cost-effective for the brand because redemption is for own products and not third-party sourced.

- When you allow for redemption against own products, even small point balances can be redeemed – this leads to higher value realised by the member. No points are "wasted" because they are too few in number

- In order to drive meaningful redemption, you can set a minimum accrual before the first redemption is allowed. E.g. first redemption is allowed only after 100 points have been accrued. Thereafter, redemption is ongoing. This helps to drive up the initial accrual and gets the ball rolling.

- When you have a catalogue for redemption, ensure that you appeal to HOARDERS and REDEEMERS. From ATTAINABLE to ASPIRATIONAL. Typically, program members are of two kinds – those who want to save for a larger reward – THE HOARDERS; And those who will keep redeeming when they have a reasonable balance – THE REDEEMERS. The catalogue must have items to cater to both. In fact, when a program is launched, most members are REDEEMERS because they want to test the program and see if promises are kept. Once trust is built, the hoarders begin to save up for larger rewards.

- Set the first milestone for redemption such that an average member is able to get a reward within 3-4 months of program membership. The quicker the first moment of truth, the more the commitment to the program.

- Have choices at each milestone – e.g. 10000 points can either get you a Bluetooth speaker or it can get you a designer knapsack. But beware of the paralysis of choice. Don't have too many options at each milestone.

- When selecting reward items for the catalogue, keep in mind the following:

  - Brands selected are in sync with the program brand and address the same/similar audience

  - When services are included, the brands offering the service must fulfil the promise (e.g. when the redemption is for a coffee and donut at Starbucks, Starbucks should accept the voucher and handle the redemption seamlessly). So brands with trust and credibility are included.

  - Items selected are based on member expectations, needs, desires. Find this out through research. Benchmark with other programs in the space. Don't offer items that add to numbers in your catalogue but have no relevance to the member base at all

- Have one or two big ticket items that will get talked about. This could be a signature brand (e.g. An Audi car) or an exclusive experience (e.g. A Holiday to an exotic location, Meeting a celebrity). Only one or two members may actually be able to attain these rewards – but they get tremendous word-of-mouth for the program attracting further membership

- Make the catalogue holistic by including charitable/do-good options – donation of points for good causes

- A relatively "easy" item for redemption these days is a voucher from e-commerce platforms like Amazon and Flipkart (in India). "Easy" because they can be procured and despatched electronically almost instantaneously. However, the important thing to remember here is that the value of the voucher is the same as the perceived value of the reward and also the cost to the brand (except for bulk purchase efficiencies)

DRIVING HIGH PERCEIVED VALUE

A true differentiator for your rewards catalogue is when you drive high perceived value or have items that are curated, items that cannot be "bought".

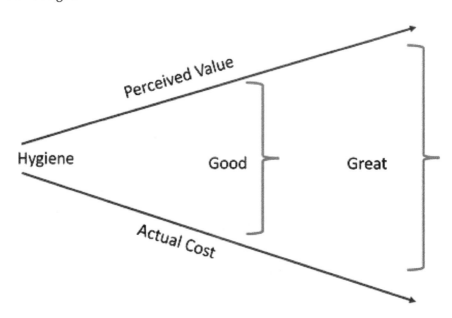

The more the difference is between the actual cost and the perceived value, the greater is the benefit for the program.

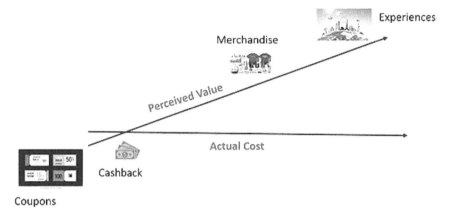

Coupons and vouchers offered by so many brands today – take the case of subscription renewal of your satellite TV plan or broadband plan – are just viewed as worthless and ignored. Their perceived value is lower than the cost you paid for them.

As you go up the value chain in terms of customisation and curation, experiential rewards and hard-to-get items, the perceived value climbs far beyond the cost to the brand.

Imagine Marriott Bonvoy offering personalised robes with the member's initials inscribed, as an item for redemption to a certain tier! Will not cost much more than the robe itself but the perceived value to the member is huge! Or Myntra Insider offers a one-on-one consultation with a top designer or brand ambassador. Imagine the virality of such an item!

REWARD ISSUANCE

There are two strategies to issue rewards:

1. AUTO ISSUANCE – when the member attains a threshold, the reward is automatically sent. This happens most often with vouchers/credit notes given by retail. This brings an element of surprise and delight as well. Saks First issues a Saks voucher

at the end of every calendar year based on the points earned in the year – and it can be used for purchases at Saks. This also means that members cannot accrue currency beyond a time. Which may or may not be good. It wipes out liability periodically and keeps the books clean, but doesn't do a great deal to drive longer term stickiness.

2. ON DEMAND – The reward is sent on the specific request of the member. Member choice and freedom dominates in this strategy. And hoarders can accrue for larger rewards.

And, finally, **measurement.** Nothing improves a reward catalogue better than analytics and measurement. Data will tell you

- Which items are popular – and at what level
- Who is redeeming, who is not
- Which items are not being redeemed at all.

While data will tell you WHAT is happening, also find out WHY – by going back to members and getting their feedback on reward options.

Reward and redemption strategy is both an art and a science. The most critical aspect is execution. A successful redemption episode creates a strong emotional connection with the brand and the program. Execute flawlessly – and if and when there is a dispute, let the customer win. Small battles may need to be lost to win the larger war.

It's not that hard!

CHAPTER 11

THE DATA VIEW FOR LOYALTY

"Think it over, think it under." Winnie the Pooh

And now, the data analytics view. Before the eyes get glazed and the tongue gets tied - first things first on expectations setting! This is not a deep-dive into data analysis. Nor is it a technical treatise on the mathematics and statistics involved in a data analytics exercise.

Data is a key input and a critical output of any loyalty initiative. This is a chapter attempting to throw light on what are the various data views required when designing for loyalty and when a program is running.

Without a data story that validates your hypotheses, it is pretty much impossible to design a good program.

Let's look at the data view from two angles:

- For program design – the Input
- Ongoing, when the program is running – the Output

DATA VIEW FOR PROGRAM DESIGN

Starting with the assumption that we have customer level transaction data available, we would ideally look at this data for a period of 24-36 months in order to identify seasonality patterns and trends across the years.

OBJECTIVES OF DATA ANALYSIS

As a precursor and input into program design, the objectives of any data analysis are primarily:

1. To identify and profile the most valuable customers (and thereby locate more of the same within the customer base)

2. To estimate headroom and areas for growth through loyalty (and use the loyalty incentives to drive desired behaviour)

3. To identify and profile customers at risk for churn (to ring fence them before the point of churn)

4. To isolate trends, patterns which can help identify gaps and opportunity areas (to leverage loyalty marketing campaigns to capitalise on these opportunities)

DATA AUDIT - STANDARDIZATION AND CLEAN-UP

One of the first steps is to undertake an AUDIT of the data available . The audit will throw light on:

- Sources – Where is the data flowing in from, are there multiple sources (e.g. online vs offline sales).

- Types of data – remember there is sales data, service data, customer complaints, customer enquiries, response to promotional offers, referrals. All these will often reside in silos within the organisation. The audit will reveal what lies where so that there is a plan to integrate whatever is possible into what is commonly called a CUSTOMER ONE VIEW

- Standardization – what fields have been captured, are they standardized across all sources

- Completeness – how much of the data is available, how much is left blank

- Quality – a random check will indicate how much of the populated data is cleaned-up and useable

Once you do the data audit, you take the necessary steps to correct lacunae and make the data ready for analysis. Where data is ingrained into an organisation and regularly used, the audit will be reasonably simple because much of the data will already be analysis-ready.

AREAS OF ANALYSIS

Let us outline broad areas of analysis that any program design may cover:

- Segmentation, Frequency Distribution

- Profiling, Range of values

- Product/Service Views

- Desired Behaviour Patterns

- Trends

- Modeling

SEGMENTATION STARTS WITH PARETO'S 80:20

One of the first analysis exercises is to do an overall Pareto. The Pareto will be based on your key business metric - e.g. revenue, frequency

In very simple, layman terms, if revenue is your key business metric, sort your customers and sales/revenue from them in a specified period (normally a year) in descending order. And then break it up into deciles. So you get a distribution of what % of sales is coming from every 10% of customers from the top to the bottom. You could do the same by frequency if frequency is your key business metric. In some cases, you would do BOTH revenue and frequency to see how customers are behaving. Are your high value customers also your high frequency customers? Or is it a totally different set that is delivering the frequency?

A basic Pareto on the key variable will immediately tell you whether your program will lend itself to tiers or not. If you find distinct breaks in the customer distribution by revenue for e.g. you will know how to structure your tiers and how many tiers will be possible. The actual decision on number of tiers will then depend on delivery capability.

RFMT

Another basic segmentation exercise normally undertaken at the start of a loyalty journey is the RFM or RFMT analysis. Score your customers on RECENCY, FREQUENCY, MONETARY VALUE AND TENURE. Assign a weightage to each of these variables. And calculate your final RFMT score per customer. This immediately identifies segments – and what you need to DO with each of the segments. As an example: with High, Medium, Low categorisation for each metric (RFM), you would end up with 27 segments - some of which are outlined below

RFM SEGMENT	TASK
HR, HF, HM	Retain and ring fence
LR, LF, LM	Ignore for the moment
LR, HF, HM	Win back
HR, LF, LM	Drive repeat, upsell
HR, MF, MM	Give reasons to transact

You may also segment your customer base in other ways:

- By product/service purchased
- By single product vs multiple products

- By tenure (years of custom) with your brand

- By demographics (if available) - age, gender, location

- By sale vs non sale periods of purchase – who are the bargain hunters vs brand seekers

VAP

Another segmentation view is the three-dimensional VALUE-ATTRITION-POTENTIAL scoring of your customer base.

Value is taken as actual revenue from the customer. Attrition scoring estimates risk of attrition - essentially, take customers who have churned, identify their characteristics through a profiling exercise and isolate others who display the same characteristics. Potential estimates future value from the customer using surrogates (like trends in transaction value) and other characteristics that have been displayed by other high value customers. This may also include geography and profile data.

The VAP framework also results in 27 different segments (assuming a High, Medium, Low for each variable) with a task for each.

Some examples below:

VAP SEGMENT	TASK
HV HP LA	Retain and grow
HV HP HA	Ring fence, build relationship
LV, LP, HA	Ignore, let them churn
LV, LP, LA	Wait and watch
LV, MP, LA	Upsell, drive behaviour

PROFILING

The next logical step after segmentation is PROFILING. Typically, you want to know what defines your Most Valuable Customers whom you will need to ring-fence. And also, what defines your Least Valuable Customers on whom you will direct least marketing investment.

Use all the relevant fields of data available at a customer level – value, transaction frequency, range, demographics, tenure, response to offers etc - and get your analytics team to profile the MVCs in terms of what are the most significant variables that defines them. For e.g. you may find that your MVCs are most likely to be those who have purchased your entire range of products. Or they are more likely to be from a certain location (e.g. Metros and Tier 1). Or your MVCs have a tenure of 5-7 years with you. This also helps you identify whom among the mid value customers are more likely to become high value.

You would do the same exercise for those at the bottom of the pyramid. This is useful in helping you identify who amongst your new customers are likely to be low value – is it defined by their entry product for e.g.?

When you profile your segments in this manner, it also helps you benchmark what are the avg, min and max range of key business metrics in each segment. For e.g. your top 5% of customers by revenue – have values of Min 100,000 INR per year, Max 550,000 INR per year and Average 225,000 INR per year. You will similarly benchmark their frequency, range and other relevant values as well. This will indicate to you what kind of tier thresholds you can set, should you decide to go in for tiers.

PRODUCT/SERVICE VIEWS

When you have a multiple product portfolio, it warrants some analysis from a product/service viewpoint as well.

You will attempt to answer questions such as:

- Who are the valuable customers by product/service? E.g. an Ecommerce marketplace like Flipkart would want to know who are their valuable mobile customers, apparel customers, appliance customers etc

- Benchmark their avg., min and max values by product/service
- Profile the valuable customers in similar fashion by product/service for more relevant targeting
- Identify whether there are any product/service combinations that are working together like a bundle

DESIRED BEHAVIOUR PATTERNS

What is "desired" behaviour from a Loyalty lens?

- Once a prospect becomes a customer (buys once), you want him/her to buy again – SECOND VISIT
- You want to drive frequency within the year – REPEAT
- You want to retain them ACROSS years – RETENTION
- You don't want them to stop buying – CHURN
- You want them to upgrade to more valuable products/services – PREMIUMISATION
- You want them to buy more than one product – RANGE

These are the key metrics for which you will look for answers from the data. This helps you identify gaps you can tackle - e.g. if 60% of your customer base is dropping out after the first transaction, one of the first tasks of loyalty is to get them to transact a second time. A premium hotel chain found that 80% of their guests stayed once and did not return. And those who did stay the second time, tended to stick with the chain. The primary task then became driving the second stay.

Data will help you identify what is the sweet spot or sticky spot after which customers are less likely to churn. Is it the third transaction? Or is it a specific product that they try?

Once you set benchmarks on these key metrics, you will know what needs to be the loyalty focus. If you are retaining only 12% of your customers year-on-year, you have a tremendously leaky bucket and loyalty must help you fix it by driving higher retention.

Are there segments like single-product loyalists? This is an opportunity area for a cross-sell.

If churn happens the greatest after the first transaction, you must target yourself to minimise churn there.

An E-commerce marketplace may find that retention is best for those customers who entered with a mobile purchase. This is a cue for what category to push as an entry.

TRENDS

Why do we analyse data over a 24-36 months period? Because one year will never tell the story. Let's say you have a product category where the average annual frequency of purchase is 1.2. E.g. jeans. With one year of data, you will not have sufficient data points to conclude anything in terms of range, repeat, churn or any of the key metrics.

Looking at data over periods of time will help you get a more realistic picture of behaviour, whilst also helping you identify seasonality or other patterns. For e.g. most fashion retailers have their EOSS (End Of Season Sale). If you observe behaviour over a couple of years, you will be able to identify and isolate a segment of buyers who are purely EOSS buyers and will respond to offers.

MODELING

And this is the beautiful simulation that only data can deliver.

Once you complete your program design in terms of tiers and thresholds, earn rates etc, you can actually model to run the program across historic data and see how it fares.

When you do this you actually get to understand what your cost vs incremental revenue implications would be, what your points liability looks like and what your tier upgrades and downgrades would result in.

A modelling exercise will then help you tweak your program structure and rules for optimum results.

ANALYTICS FOR ONGOING PROGRAM

Once your program is running it begins to throw out critical data which you can then analyse to tweak, fine-tune and drive metrics further.

Data analysis helps to drive

1. EFFICIENCY – Do more with less, do it quicker, lower your business risk
2. INTELLIGENCE – Make better, more empowered decisions, target more relevantly, improve conversions, drive better metrics

OBJECTIVES OF DATA ANALYTICS FOR A RUNNING PROGRAM

- Evaluate program performance against set objectives and deliverables
- Evaluate effectiveness of program structure
- Assess overall program health, performance, significance and long-term viability

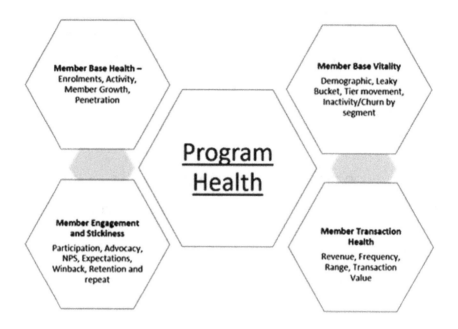

Questions that program data will help answer will broadly fall into 4 areas:

MEMBER BASE HEALTH

- Are your program enrolments growing y-o-y?

- What is the activity level of your member base? (Activity defined as per the business as a certain number of transactions in a specified period)

- What is the total value of sales coming from your member base and is this growing?

- What % of total sales of your brand is coming from the program and is this penetration improving?

MEMBER BASE VITALITY

- What is the demographic distribution of your member base?

- How many new members are being enrolled vs members who have dropped out? Do you have a leaky bucket?

- If you have tiers in your program, what are the upgrades and downgrades like? Are downgrades more than upgrades (cause for concern)? Are upgrades more than downgrades (is your program structure stable)?
- Is any one tier bloating more than others?

MEMBER TRANSACTION HEALTH

- What are the key metrics of members? Overall and by segment/ tier – Average Transaction Value, Average Revenue per member, Average Frequency per member, Range
- Are these metrics improving or are there some which are stagnant/declining?
- How do these metrics compare with those of non-members?
- What are the min and max values of these metrics by segment/ tier?

MEMBER STICKINESS AND ENGAGEMENT

- What is the churn rate and is this declining?
- What is the member retention rate y-o-y?
- Have activity levels improved by segment?
- Are members participating in program activities?
- How responsive are members to communication, offers?
- Are members referring others?
- What is the sweet spot/sticky spot after which churn declines and members tend to stay with the program and brand?
- What are member expectations?
- What are the member satisfaction levels and what is the Net Promoter Score?

Data analysis is truly the engine that helps design better programs and also keeps them true to their purpose. Ensure you have a good analytics team to support you during design and as an integral part of the ongoing program management team.

As a program manager it is not necessary to KNOW the mathematical and statistical tools or how to operate the analytics software. Your analytics team is there to support and lead that function. What is important is to be AWARE of the data that exists and what are the insights you want to generate out of the analysis.

Ask the right questions and let the analytics do the magic! It's not that hard.

CHAPTER 12

LOYALTY PROGRAM BRANDING AND COMMUNICATION

"The most wonderful thing about Tiggers is, I'm the only one." — Tigger, Winnie the Pooh

A study in the US many years ago showed that the key reason for the failure and closure of loyalty programs was – not rewards, not the earn rate, not the privileges – it was simply the absolute LACK of communication from program to member.

As George Bernard Shaw famously said – "The biggest single problem with communication is the ILLUSION that it has taken place"!

And this is a fate that befalls many programs even today. There is a surfeit of communication as you launch, as you enrol members – which then peters out and fades into nothingness. The attitude seems to be : *The members are already in, they can find out what the program offers and they can earn and redeem when they choose. What's to communicate?*

Nothing can be further from the truth. If you don't communicate with your members, you are simply taking them for granted. Yes, over-communication is a huge irritation and fatigue factor but swinging the other way is like signing your program's death warrant.

What's the best way to handle this?

Let's look at this from two aspects:

1. Branding
2. Communication

BRANDING

Unlike product marketing and advertising where so much importance is given to the careful creation of a BRAND that will last a lifetime, not enough significance is given to loyalty program branding as it should. It is almost by default that the program name often becomes "Brand Name+ Club/Circle/Family/Rewards Etc". While this is not a bad way to go and no one wants creativity for its own sake, it is worth thinking about what we can do to create a lasting program brand.

There are THREE branding opportunities within a loyalty program that can be leveraged for greater mileage and salience.

- PROGRAM NAME
- CURRENCY NAME
- TIER NAMES

Let's look at some of the well-known programs and their names:

- STARBUCKS
  - Program – My Starbucks Rewards
  - Currency – Stars
  - Tiers – Welcome, Green, Gold
- SEPHORA
  - Program- Beauty Insider
  - Currency – Points

- Tiers – Insider, VIB (Very Important Beauty Insider), Rouge
- NEIMAN MARCUS/BERGDORF GOODMAN
  - Program – InCircle
  - Currency – Points
  - Tiers – Circles 1 to 6, President's Circle, Chairman's Circle
- NORDSTROM
  - Program - The Nordy Club
  - Currency – Points and Nordstrom Notes
  - Tiers – Member, Influencer, Ambassador

Closer home….

- SHOPPERS STOP
  - Program – First Citizen Club
  - Currency – Points
  - Tiers – Silver Edge, Golden Glow, Platinum Aura, Black
- FABINDIA
  - Program – FabFamily
  - Currency – FabCoins
  - Tiers – Bronze, Silver, Gold, Platinum, Black
- TATA NEU
  - Program – Tata Neu
  - Currency – Neu Coins
  - No tiers as yet
- FLIPKART
  - Program – Flipkart Plus
  - Currency – SuperCoins
  - No tiers as yet

- VISTARA
  - Program – Club Vistara
  - Currency – CV Points
  - Tiers – Base, Silver, Gold, Platinum

Other striking and renowned program brand names include – AMAZON PRIME or PRIME (as well-recalled as Amazon itself), MARRIOTT BONVOY, erstwhile JET PRIVILEGE which then became INTERMILES; ZILLION – erstwhile PAYBACK – India's first open Coalition program; Programs that got integrated into Tata Neu – TITAN ENCIRCLE, TAJ INNER CIRCLE… and many more.

What seems to be a common factor across all is that, program brand names are given some thought so that they reflect the parent brand and ethos. Thereafter, the trend is to keep Currency and Tier names fairly simple – and obvious.

BRANDING PRINCIPLES:

- Leverage the opportunity to create memorable brand names that stand the test of time – for the program, currency and tiers

- However, don't complicate for the sake of innovation. Tier and currency names do need to be simple and fairly obvious for easy remembrance - so, create within that framework

- The program brand must reflect the parent brand in tone, manner and ethos. Look and feel needs to immediately connect with the parent brand.

- Invest in marketing the program brand so that it has salience – Shoppers Stop and First Citizen Club are equally well recognised. So also Amazon and Amazon Prime.

- Have a distinguishing logo and tag line – and use this logo unit in all program communication

- If your currency has greater possibilities of salience then leverage that. Flipkart SuperCoins has become a well-established property because the coins are widely fungible – as much as or perhaps more than Flipkart Plus, their loyalty program.

- Tier names must connote the elevation in status with enhanced rewards, benefits, privileges and recognition. So a Silver, Gold, Platinum does work. Except that it has become almost ubiquitous so some exploration to establish a different identity for tiers may actually work in the program's favour.

- Typically a program brand must reflect – affinity, benefits, long-term relationship

COMMUNICATION

"It is more fun to talk with someone who doesn't use long, difficult words but rather short, easy words like, 'What about lunch?'" — *Winnie the Pooh*

Why the specific focus on loyalty communication? Isn't it pretty much the same as brand communication?

There are some subtle and not-so-subtle differences between Marketing Communication and Loyalty Communication.

Brand Marketing Communication

- In most cases, targets the audience as a mass

- Uses broad demographics and psychographics as cues

- Uses above-the-line media, mass media

- Focuses on customer acquisition, creating brand recognition and salience

- Is normally one-way and follows a "push" model

Loyalty Communication

- Targets the audience as focused segments, even a segment-of-one

- Uses individual customer data – behavioural, transactional, profile

- Uses one-to-one media

- Focuses on customer retention and development, demands action

- Is two-way and dialogue based. It aims at building an ongoing relationship. Always. Or it should be!

Loyalty program communications start out with several advantages:

- The member has consented to program membership – and therefore is open to receive information from the program

- There is tremendous opportunity to pinpoint and drive relevance because you KNOW the customer at an individual level – you know his/her behaviour with you, you know his/her history with you.

- You can create reasons to talk to and listen to the member. You can create moments of truth.

COMMUNICATION PLAN

There are four basic principles to follow in designing your communication plan:

1. **Segmentation and Targeting.** Your program membership base is not a homogenous mass. Avoid carpet bombing even if the argument is that the per contact cost is low! The cost of fatigue and resistance to your communication in future, is high. Target your communication based on meaningful segments. Segments can be basis obvious variables like age, gender, geography (for city-based offers) or program tier. To drive more meaning it is

important to have nuanced segmentation based on behaviour (transactional and non-transactional), lifecycle and milestones, earn and involvement levels, responsiveness and participation, social media action. Use variables in combination for better effect. Today's technology allows you to target a segment of one – leverage the ability.

2. **Drive Relevance and Relationship** – The whole idea of segmentation is that you then use the information about the member to speak to him relevantly and build a relationship. The content – messaging and offer - will vary based on segment characteristics. You KNOW the member, you know the history, you have a multi-dimensional view. Tailor-make your communication based on what you know. Relevance is what opens emails and prompts action. And as the member acts, you get to know more and can fine-tune your communication accordingly. Keep the dialog going.

3. **Action Orientation** – One-to-one communication must be action oriented. It is different from mass media advertising in that sense. Awareness and perception creation are not the only objectives here. It is important to drive some response, some action – even if it is a raising of hand saying "I'm interested". There must be a strong call to action and your layout and copy must be geared for that.

4. **Permission Based** – Most important principle and a best practice. Ask actively for access before you communicate. Don't hide the terms and conditions in small print. And don't use the negative option *("unless you say no, I'm going to communicate")*. Honour all opt-out requests. Ensure 100% compliance to data privacy regulations. If you have multiple brands and the customer is a member of one of your brand programs, it does not automatically mean that other brands in your stable can communicate with that member – unless permission is explicitly sought. This may reduce the communicable base –

but helps drive your other objectives of relevance and action orientation. Besides building member goodwill!

A loyalty communication plan will be two pronged and based on:

- Where the PROGRAM is in its lifecycle

- Where the MEMBER is in his/her membership cycle with the brand

There are three broad buckets of communication:

- **Program Related** – This will include Solicitation and enrolment, Welcome kit/Welcome message, program features and benefits, Program News and updates, Program newsletter, Redemption Catalogue, New partners etc. This will be based on both the program lifecycle and member lifecycle.

- **Behaviour Driving** – this will be based on the segments you have – examples would be – "You're almost at the next tier", "We missed you, you haven't come for long", "You are close to being downgraded", "You have xyz points available for redemption – here are some great items to redeem for", "You bought this last time, here's another colour", "Special offer on this item for this month", "Refer a friend", "Fill up your profile information", "Your membership is dormant, activate it before" ....there can be many, many more examples based on the behaviour you want to drive

- **Relationship/Recognition** – This will largely be goodwill and relationship building communication based on the program lifecycle and the member lifecycle. This is a very important component of any loyalty communication plan. "It's our 10th anniversary! Here's a special offer". "Happy Birthday/ Anniversary/Festival" "Congratulations you've reached 10,000 points, here's a gift for you" "This is a social cause your program is associated with, would you want to participate" "We are now at 50,000 members, thank you all!" "We have a member benefit show coming up, here is your invitation" "Seeking your feedback, tell us what you think of…" " You are important to us, will you be part of a member suggestion panel"

For each segment you will then prioritise - what communication will go out, when/how often in the year, through what channels (email, sms, WhatsApp, physical mail, event). If you over-communicate, you run the risk of fatigue and disinterest. If you under-communicate, there is a risk of the member forgetting the program exists. How do you bring about a balance?

You have a WATERFALL with rules: e.g. You will NOT communicate more than twice a week to the Platinum member. Between a birthday wish and a marketing targeted message that will go out, the birthday wish gets priority. Profile updates are requested only twice a year. Between a program newsletter and a special offer in the same week, the offer gets priority… etc etc. These are examples of how you will prioritise based on the goals set for the program.

Curate a communication plan by segment for a period of 12 months. Allow for some flexibility every month/quarter because there are always brand priorities you have to keep in mind. Have a balance of channels used though you would restrict physical/ face-to-face events only for your most valuable customers given the cost and logistics involved.

And finally, keep in mind the RULE OF 3:

- Tell them what you're going to do
- Tell them you're doing it
- Tell them what you just did

No place for bashfulness here!

It's not that hard…

CHAPTER 13

PROGRAM PARTNERSHIPS

"You can't stay in your corner of the Forest waiting for others to come to you. You have to go to them sometimes." — *Winnie the Pooh*

When we studied the different program models we talked of Proprietary programs and how they evolve into Partner programs over time to enhance the value proposition. There are also cases of some programs which are launched as partner programs in their primary proposition.

Do all programs need to have partners? No. If your program has enough to offer its members in terms of variety, velocity and engagement, you can pretty much run your program on the back of your brand and program promise.

Bringing in partners has its own risk. You are now dependent on another set of brand/s to uphold and deliver on your program promise. If there is a genuine need, opportunity and you have the leverage to negotiate based on your program strengths, only then will you consider partners.

Adding partners is an OPM strategy. Other People's Money cascading into the program. When relevant and smartly done, this tremendously improves the program's financial viability.

JOURNEY TO PARTNERSHIP PROGRAMS

While some programs do launch as partner programs, typically the journey starts with a proprietary program that then begins to add partners as it evolves.

Let us quickly revisit the basic principles of a Partner Program

- The program is still OWNED by the parent brand that is seeking partners

- Partners are tied in either for earn of program currency, burn (redemption) of program currency or both – or they can be tied in to make tangible offers to the program member base.

- The currency liability is held with the parent program brand

- There are individual agreements with each partner – principal to principal – which will specify the rate of currency issuance and currency redemption

- When the partner ISSUES your brand program currency to their customers, they will pay the program brand at a per currency unit rate for ISSUANCE

- When program currency is REDEEMED at the partner outlet, then the program brand compensates the partner for the redeemed currency at a pre-agreed value for currency REDEMPTION

- Sensible financial principles will mean that the ISSUANCE rate is higher than the REDEMPTION rate and the arbitrage between issuance and redemption rate is an earn for the program owner.

If a typical program evolution cycle is followed, then the program will first tie up EARN partners who will issue the program currency while BURN is restricted within the program brand ecosystem. Sensible financial practice because Earn is an inflow and Burn is an outflow for the program. The partnership then evolves to burn partners and then finally to partners who are both earn and burn. This is however not a hard and fast rule. It depends - as always – on the program priorities.

Quick point of note here – structurally, a partnership program is different from a COALITION. In a Coalition, the program and the currency are owned by a third-party entity that has an arm's length distance with the partners/sponsors.

WHY WOULD BRANDS WANT TO TIE-UP AS PARTNERS FOR AN EXISTING PROGRAM?

There are several reasons why brands are keen to enter into partnership agreements with existing programs.

- They don't have the financial and infrastructure wherewithal to run their own program
- They don't have either the variety or the velocity to sustain a program on their own
- They are looking for customer acquisition - and this becomes as quick way of attracting customers if the program brand and currency are popular.
- It adds to the value proposition they are offering their customers vs their competitors – and helps gain market share
- They get data insights of individual customers transacting with the program - which they would otherwise not get

BENEFITS TO THE PROGRAM BRAND

- Tangible addition to the program value proposition

- Adds "interest" and "relevance" – especially so if the category is dull and lacks excitement and novelty

- Adds earn velocity. Choosing partners carefully helps drive earn velocity. Take a category like automobiles. Once the car is purchased and the currency is earned, there is very little interaction with the brand or program - very few "earn" opportunities. Adding a partner who will help drive earn velocity will improve member-program engagement - partners may be accessories, fuel and lubes, even travel partners - especially those suited for road travel

- Partners, if added with strategic intent, become a key program differentiator adding tremendous value

- And, most importantly, financial viability and sustainability. The moment there are others issuing the currency, the program begins to earn on issuance and the earn-burn arbitrage adds to the program bottom line.

TYPES OF PARTNER ENGAGEMENTS

Partner engagements and tenets of agreements drawn with them will differ depending on the commitments offered.

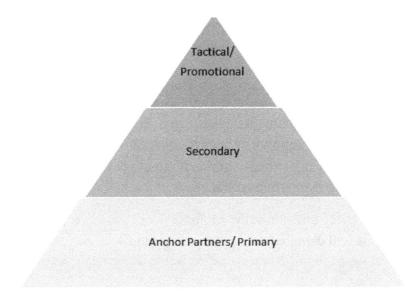

Type of Partner	Tenure	Offering	Financial Arrangement	Exclusivity	Media and exposure	Data Insights
Primary/Anchor	3-5 years	Earn, burn, special solutions	Min commitment, special rates	Yes - category and sub-category	Committed, part of all program communication, program logo	Customised and ongoing
Secondary	1 year	Earn or Burn	Lower commitment, rates not negotiated	Yes – category	Committed – but lower than anchor	Restricted
Tactical	Quarterly	Promotions and offers	No financial engagement	No	None	None

As a program evolves into a Partnership model, there are different kinds of engagement models with prospective partners.

ANCHOR PARTNERS

These are strategic and longer-term tie-ups. Such partners are normally granted exclusivity within the category/sub-category. The program and the partner invest in creating special products/ services/ solutions for the member base that will add value to the program brand and the partner brand.

For a certain minimum commitment from the partner on issuance of currency, they will be given a specially negotiated issuance rate. Normally anchor partners are both earn and burn.

There are special agreements drawn on sharing of data insights (assuming all permissions are taken from the members). Program brand and communication will feature the anchor partner name and the partner will have a certain number of guaranteed communication contacts with the program member base.

Anchor partners are normally singular – or two at a maximum. Agreements will usually be for a 3-5 year period.

A co-branded program credit-card is an anchor partner arrangement with the issuing bank.

SECONDARY PARTNERS

Secondary partners are tied-in for a shorter period – normally a year. All conditions of partnership are restricted when compared to the primary partners and the financial commitment from secondary partners is also lower.

Secondary partners may be either earn or burn – unlikely that they will be allowed both earn and burn. Limited data insights are shared.

There may be multiple secondary partners tied up, with minimal exclusivity. If at all exclusivity is offered, it will be for the broader category – not sub category.

Hotel programs may have annual tie-ups with related services like car rentals or airlines.

TACTICAL/PROMOTIONAL PARTNERS

These are quickly executed tie-ups where partner brands make offers to the program member base. They are shorter period arrangements – perhaps a quarter / maybe even a month. No data insights are shared – this just becomes a quick-fix means of brand salience and acquisition for the partner brand. There are no earn-burn arrangements with tactical partners. It is a quick and simple promotion.

The plenitude of offers you are asked to click on when you renew your DTH or Broadband subscription is an example of promotional partnerships.

The program may choose to go ahead with any or all of the above partner engagement models – in any combination - depending on the need of the hour.

PARTNER SELECTION

The critical factors in selection of partners are **complementarity of category** and **synergy of brand.**

Let's look at two dimensions for category complementarity.

- Frequency/ Velocity of earn
- Margin/ Volume of earn

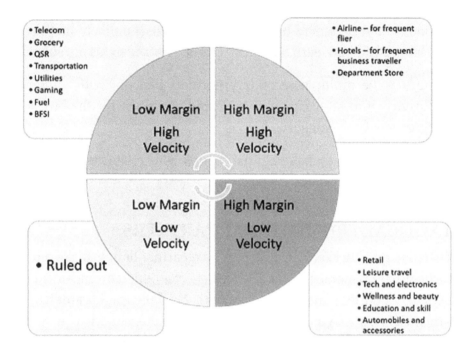

These are just examples of categories that fall into each quadrant. The first step is to identify which quadrant your brand falls into. Thereafter, decide whether you want to ENHANCE what you are already offering (e.g. increase velocity of earn) or choose a category with a complementary offering – e.g. you offer high velocity, choose a category which has high margin to afford a greater giveback.

Once you have a shortlist of CATEGORIES that you will target for partnerships, the next step is to prioritise BRANDS that your program can associate with. Here is a short set of guiding principles (especially for Anchor and Secondary partners).

Choose brands that:

- Address the same target audience as your brand
- Have a similar brand personality, tone and manner – e.g. if your brand has a fun and vibrant personality, try and choose similar brands.
- Are reasonably large and have loyal customer bases themselves; caveat - some brands are niche brands with a small but loyal customer base- that makes immense sense too.
- Are known to keep their brand promise with customers
- Are good on on-ground delivery – this is a big moment of truth
- Will be financially viable for you – so the commercial arrangement has to make sense for your program

Partners are a good way to enhance a program value proposition and also parallelly make the program more sustainable as well as drive greater stickiness with members.

The important criterion is to pick the right partners and make the right partnership agreements which are fair to the program brand and the partner brand.

A guideline in selecting the right brands with category adjacencies as well as personality synergy would be to do a quick check with members on the brands they use across categories and also what partnerships would add value to them.

Simple enough? It's not that hard!

CHAPTER 14

LOYALTY PROGRAM FINANCIAL MODELING

"Managing your finances is like being a chef – you have to carefully balance the ingredients to create a delicious and satisfying outcome." Anon

What are the payoffs from my loyalty program?

When will it start making money?

What are the investments I will have to make?

What if I didn't do a program, what would the results be?

Is it going to be worth it?

These are some of the questions we will address in this chapter on Financial Modeling for Loyalty.

But, first, important to set some basic expectations.

It is an indefatigable and undisputed truth that loyalty WORKS. Proven by several studies globally and seen by loyalty marketers, loyalty initiatives, done properly, will pay-off and they are critically needed. We have discussed earlier that acquiring a new customer is several times more expensive that retaining and growing your existing customers. So, there should be no doubt about the financial pay-offs of loyalty.

It is also an undisputed fact that loyalty is a medium to long-term strategy. It takes time, effort, investment – and it may or may not produce immediate results. You want short-term profit spikes? Loyalty is not your answer. You need to have the faith, the commitment and the staying power for you to see it reap substantial results for you. Plan, execute, evaluate, fine-tune, continue to stay the course. And you will see the benefits. There's no two ways about it.

The key question to ask therefore is not "Will I make money from Loyalty?" The question really is "How do I drive profitable behavioural change in a financially sustainable business model?"

We need to look at financial modelling for loyalty from two lenses:

1. What is the INCREMENTAL benefit a loyalty program delivers (over and above natural growth scenarios)?

2. What is the OPPORTUNITY COST of not running a loyalty initiative?

The Loyalty Equation in its simplest form is:

INCREMENTAL REVENUE – INCREMENTAL COST = INCREMENTAL PROFIT

Let's now break this down and understand it further.

COMPONENTS OF INCREMENTAL REVENUE

We typically speak of three effects of running a loyalty program:

1. The LIFT effect

2. The RETENTION effect

3. The SHIFT effect

The LIFT EFFECT refers to the LIFT or improvement in desired behaviour metrics as a result of the loyalty initiative. There are two basic components of revenue – the number of times a transaction is done and the amount spent per transaction. So, we are referring to HIGHER TRANSACTION VALUE and HIGHER FREQUENCY leading to HIGHER REVENUE PER CUSTOMER because of Loyalty.

The RETENTION EFFECT refers to members staying longer with your brand as a result of loyalty. This is measured by the REDUCTION IN MEMBER CHURN . When members stay longer than they would NORMALLY have done, and continue to spend with your brand, this is incremental revenue generated by the program.

The SHIFT EFFECT refers to new acquisition as a result of loyalty. Which means, new **customers** are acquired by the brand because of the halo effect of the program. This is normally a "bonus" offshoot and not a primary deliverable of loyalty. When you have a long-standing and high performing program, it attracts new customers to the brand – but this takes a long time period and is not typically a short-term or medium-term result. One way to look at the SHIFT effect, however, is to consider existing customers who start joining the program as members and are then impacted by the program initiatives. So, program new enrolments are also a reflection of the SHIFT effect.

COMPONENTS OF INCREMENTAL COST

Incremental cost essentially refers to the cost of running the loyalty initiative – this is apart from regular marketing and branding costs.

Typically, the bulk of this would be the "giveback" to the member in terms of points. The other significant costs would be – special benefits and privileges/services given to members, loyalty communications, loyalty fulfilment, loyalty infrastructure and support services, loyalty analytics, loyalty team manpower costs etc. Some of these costs are FIXED costs amortised over 3-5 years – e.g. the cost of a loyalty system. The rest would be monthly/annual variable costs which would depend on the member base.

We now look at a step-by-step process for building a loyalty model. And remember, this is an iterative process and you will have re-assess and revise your assumptions several times before you come to a model that will give a reasonably true picture.

MEMBER BASE SIZING

The first step in Program Financial Modeling is sizing your member base. Projections of member base are estimates based on previous learning and past experience – and ratified using data analysis. This is important. Use data wherever you can.

In a very simplified form:

- Estimate the size of your CUSTOMER base. If you have customer level transaction data, you already know this. If you don't, you have to make judgement calls based on surrogate data like number of bills - and overlay this with frequency assumptions. Asking your field staff to ratify these assumptions is a good call, because they have the best pulse on the customer.

- Segment your customer base, based on data, into **base, good, better and best customers**. The thumb rule is generally a distribution of 40:30:20:10 but your data will give you a better answer

- Now add a filter of CONTACTABILITY of your customer base (whether at the store or through communication). Let's say you are able to contact about 80% of this base that you have estimated. This will vary by brand and the state of customer data available in the system. You may also have different contactability rates by segment.

- Now project enrolment from each of these segments – enrolment rates will be highest for your BEST customers because they are the ones who will derive the best value from the program. Enrolment rates progressively decrease by segment – lowest for the base segment. Also keep in mind that your enrolment rates depend on your eligibility criteria and enrolment strategy which we discussed earlier. Let's say you are AUTO ENROLLING everyone, then your contactable customer base is basically your member base as well. We also studied that auto-enrolment leads to larger member bases but lower activity levels – so this is a filter you will have to apply later in the model!

- You now have a projected member base by segment. And therefore, a total member base for the program

- In a multi-year model, you will now have to project member bases for subsequent years using two variables:

  - New enrolments into the program by segment – again this depends on your eligibility criteria and enrolment strategy

  - Member churn from one year to the next.

- You would further fine-tune sizing if your program has tiers – instead of the four segments, you will now introduce tiers.

- There are a lot of assumptions to be made – but using judgement, ratified by data where available and benchmarking / field force calls, is a good enough start which you can fine-tune as you go along.

- You now have the model starting point. MEMBER BASE BY YEAR for the next three years.

MODEL WITH "NO PROGRAM"

The next step is to build a base case model where there is NO PROGRAM running. Which means, all you have is the current scenario continuing with marketing initiatives as planned for the brand.

This is done for YEAR 0 and YEAR 1. YEAR 0 is the base year and YEAR 1 is the first year we are planning for.

For building this base case model, you need the following:

1. Customer base for YEAR 0 - from data

2. Customer base for YEAR 1 – estimating natural growth in customer base based on historical data trends.

3. Revenue from this customer base in YEAR 0 – from data

4. Projected revenue from the Year 1 customer base in Year 1 – assuming growth in member transaction value and member frequency from historical trends. This is done by segment – base, good, better, best.

This is the base figure we are benchmarking against for the loyalty model.

YEAR 1 – WITH PROGRAM

We now begin to model for the first year of running the program. YEAR 1.

1. We start with member base projected for Year 1 (from member sizing above)

2. Remember that the program will impact metrics **only of the member base** and not the total customer base.

3. In a no-program scenario, with only natural growth considered, arrive at the revenue per **projected member** using the member transaction value and frequency from the NO PROGRAM scenario above. This is done by segment – Base, Good, Better, Best. **This will then give you the total revenue from the projected member base if there was no program.**

4. Now begin to assume lifts. Lift in Frequency and lift in Average Transaction Value (ATV). Assumptions are made based on past experience in the category, benchmarking with others, best practices etc. A cue - remember, it is easier to lift ATV than it is to lift frequency - once a member comes to shop, targeted efforts can help drive the value of the transaction up. It is more difficult to get them to shop more often – though that is also a

key loyalty deliverable. So, make your lift assumptions with care. You now have a new frequency and ATV per member leading to a new revenue per member – and therefore total revenue from the member base. Again, this is done by segment.

5. **Incremental revenue generated by the program – Point 4 (-) Point 3.**

Layer this simplistic model described above with:

- Member acquisition projections by month (instead of an annual figure) - so you have monthly revenue from the program. Especially important in YEAR 1 as it takes time for the program to gain traction

- Assumptions of lift can be in a range of OPTIMISTIC, REALISTIC and PESSIMISTIC. This gives you a view of the range you are operating with.

- Adding other ingredients of incremental revenue – e.g. referrals and new memberships, higher transaction values during redemption transactions etc

- You can dovetail with marketing plans and add lifts generated by new product trials, new SKU introduced etc

- If you're charging a membership fee as part of your strategy, this is another revenue line item

As you add more nuances, the model becomes more and more sensitive and tends towards realistic numbers to expect.

This is the revenue side of the model.

Next is to look at costs

PROGRAM COSTS

The biggest cost impact in a currency program will come from issuance of currency. As a thumb rule, a GOOD program is where 60-65% of cost in YEAR 1 is "given back" to the members in the form of points, benefits, privileges, communication, events etc.

CURRENCY ISSUANCE

We have already discussed, in detail, the currency strategy. We now build it into the model.

Let's assume your program is giving 5% back as points or miles. The first line item in your costs is POINTS EARN accounted for as 5% of revenue from the program member base. This is again calculated at a per member level, by segment, and then aggregated.

As we discussed earlier on Currency Strategy – you can break up currency earn into Base Earn and Bonus Earn and build both in the model. List down all the instances of Bonus earn planned for. For bonus earn you may have to include a filter of how many members will perform the desired behaviour (e.g. new product trial or one additional visit etc) and therefore become eligible for the bonus.

Now take a look at the **per member earn** that you arrive at. What is the average earn, the minimum earn and the maximum earn and do these numbers look attractive enough whilst being affordable for the program? Can an average member get a reasonable reward on redemption and how long will this award take to attain? Take an experienced call and revisit the line items if required

ACCOUNTING FOR CURRENCY ISSUANCE

The best person to handle currency accounting for loyalty is someone with actuarial qualifications. It is a precise and in-depth science and requires considerable expertise.

This book does not get into financial accounting of currency in detail.

However, here are some basic principles to remember:

- Currency issuance is a LIABILITY. It is not a cash outflow for the program. It is treated as deferred revenue which will be realised when the points are redeemed.

- Currency that is REDEEMED is cost that is incurred and hence an outflow.

- Currency that expires (not redeemed) - BREAKAGE - is realised revenue that flows back to your bottom line because you have already accounted for it.

- Programs have to follow specific regulations for accounting of currency. The regulation states that you must have holdings equal to the value of currency issuance (less the estimated breakage) so that you are able to fulfil the promise of redemptions whenever they happen. There are case study examples in the US where airlines like Delta and United have accumulated points liability in millions of dollars - such that, if all the members were to come to redeem their points at the same time, the airlines would not survive!!

- One way is to account for it at full value – much like a marketing expense. So if 5% of revenue is issued as currency, the whole amount is taken as cost for the year. In that case, it is not in your liability account. It is a marketing expense. This is a safe and conservative method because you are not ballooning your liability. Most programs don't do this however because it has a huge impact on the cost line and the program is unlikely to look profitable for a while. Very few CFOs will agree to this because it is a fact that all points don't get redeemed.

- The other way is to account for it at what is designated as FAIR VALUE after accounting for breakage. Let's say, you have planned for a currency validity of 6 months and you expect breakage of 40%. Then you account only for 60% of the currency issued – and not at "face value" but at FAIR VALUE which is really cost to the company plus a fair margin. This FAIR VALUE of all currency issued is a deferred revenue holding in your liability account.

- If you have set currency validity at 12 months or more, remember, there will be no breakage in YEAR 1 because currency does not expire till the beginning of YEAR 2. You account for the full currency issued at fair value in YEAR 1.

- YEAR 2 onwards breakage will begin to occur – remember that redemption always follows the FIFO principle – First In First Out - currency earned FIRST is redeemed FIRST.

  - Let's look at a member who has earned currency as follows (in INR Values) – MONTH 1 – 300, MONTH 4 – 700, MONTH 8 – 500. Total earned in 12 months – 1500 INR

  - He redeems in MONTH 6 – 500. This means the MONTH 1 300 and 200 from MONTH 4 have been redeemed.

  - He redeems again in MONTH 9 – 600. This means balance 500 from MONTH 4 and 100 from MONTH 6 are redeemed.

  - What is left is 400 INR – earned in Month 8 – and hence due for expiry 12 months from Month 8. So, the first breakage for this member will occur then if the currency is not redeemed.

  - This will be similarly accounted for on a per member account and then aggregated to arrive at redemptions monthly and breakage monthly.

- Other costs have to be then accounted for:

  - Program technology – fixed (for the system and engine) and variable (for maintenance and updates every year)

  - Mobile app and website development for the program - and maintenance of the same annually

  - Program infrastructure and support services – call centre, fulfilment centre etc

- Program communication – strictly cost for only loyalty communication that goes to members – not for brand communication etc

- Program reward costs and vendor management – negotiating smartly for rewards is a huge factor in driving profitability for programs.

- Program benefits and services – whether it is lounge access or separate check in counter or a separate teller at retail outlets or a special relationship manager or free delivery – all these are costs

- Events and privileges planned for – a birthday cake sent to all platinum members costs money and needs to be accounted for

- Program Analytics – this may be separate from marketing analytics – hardware, software, people costs

- Program Management and Operations - there may be an in-house team or a service provider agency for this

- Program Manpower – the in-house loyalty team

Normally loyalty tech system costs are amortised over a three to five year period

You may choose to allocate some of these costs to internal systems/ teams already running so that you don't needlessly burden the loyalty program from the start. The marketing department may absorb some of these costs as expenses.

You now have :

- Incremental Revenue elements for Year 1

- Incremental Costs for Year 1

- The difference tells you whether you are making money from Loyalty in Year 1

Chances are you will not. And if you believe your assumptions of member sizing, lifts and costs are reasonable, don't change them just to make the model look good.

Loyalty is not meant to make money from year 1 and the organisation needs to have the stomach and the wherewithal to absorb the costs for larger pay-offs in the medium and long term.

YEAR 2 ONWARDS

As you move into Year 2 and further, you will now refine the model with reasonable and informed assumptions of:

- SIZING
  - How many members are retained from the previous year
  - Therefore, how many have churned – remember that loyalty impacts churn positively – fewer members will churn than would have otherwise
  - How many new members will enrol
  - Your member base will therefore comprise two components – existing members and new members – and the impact of loyalty will vary for each
  - You may introduce tiering – which will replace the base, good, better, best segments. This will mean modelling for tier sizing as well as tier movements - upgrades and downgrades – in the following years.
- INCREMENTAL REVENUE
  - ATV and frequency lifts which will be higher than Year 1 – remember to nuance the model with different lifts for new members and existing members – and by tier/segment.
  - Shift effect through program word-of-mouth and referral generation
  - Additional revenue from redemption transactions

- Currency breakage
- INCREMENTAL COSTS
  - Currency issuance – and redemption – this may vary by tier.
  - Costs of new initiatives planned
  - All other cost lines

As you fine-tune the revenue and cost sides of the model for the following years, you will begin to see how loyalty makes money for you!

MONETISING LOYALTY PROGRAMS AND DRIVING HIGHER VALUE

As your program evolves, you will begin to look at streams of revenue that will help monetise your program.

1. Membership Fees – if you are already not charging a fee, you may choose to introduce a fee or a paid variant or a paid tier. This becomes a new revenue line.

2. Partnerships and Licensing of currency – Tying up partners who will issue your currency is a big revenue stream. Every time the partner issues your currency to their customers, they pay the program for the currency issued at a pre-agreed rate

3. Data, MIS, Insights – for partners - depending on partnership agreements you can charge for data and insights that the program delivers to partners

4. Access to database for communication – while the program will never share the database, they may provide access to the database for partners to send out promotional communication at a cost. This is, of course, assuming that member permissions have been taken

5. Changing currency value – not recommended unless absolutely required. But this is another way to monetise programs. If the value of the currency changes from INR 1 per coin to INR 0.75p per coin, your liability in the deferred revenue holding immediately drops as well. The same can be done with currency rates agreed upon with partners

6. Redemption drives to wipe out liability – periodic drives to drive redemption not only improves the liability but also improves overall program health

7. Introduce bonus currency with limited validity – e.g. a birthday bonus just for the month of the birthday. It drives redemption transactions and higher value.

8. Bonuses sponsored by partners – they issue targeted bonuses of your currency to their customers for a specific period – again this can have limited validity. The partners win and so does the program

9. Better reward negotiations – this is relevant where rewards are from a catalogue – e.g. credit card programs – improved negotiations to source rewards at lower rates whilst keeping the perceived value high, impacts program profitability positively

10. Driving aspiration and perceived value – curated rewards and experiences which may not cost much but are viewed as extremely desirable because they are so personalised and relevant, helps drive program value higher

Building a program financial model is a painstaking and iterative exercise. Allow for time and plenty of discussions – heated arguments even! Don't be afraid of making assumptions – you have to start somewhere and putting down a gut number is a good way to start.

It takes effort, it is excruciatingly time-consuming – but really, it's not that hard!

CHAPTER 15

PROGRAM METRICS AND MEASUREMENT

"It would be so nice if something made sense for a change." Alice In
Wonderland

The fundamental question: "Is my program working for me?".

A part of this question has been answered in the chapter on Data
View For Loyalty.

You can answer this question only by having a cadenced and
systematic measurement plan that measures the RIGHT variables,
at the RIGHT time and by the RIGHT methods. All three factors are
important. You need to know what to measure, at what frequency
and what is the best way to measure it.

Let's first address the often-touted accusation about measurement of
the effectiveness of loyalty – **THE SELF-SELECTION BIAS.**

What is the SELF-SELECTION BIAS? It is the hypothesis that since
loyalty programs really benefit your regular (valuable) customers, it
is they who will choose to join ("self-selection"), perform under the

program, respond to program initiatives - and hence the metrics of program members will always be better than the metrics of the rest of the customer base. This is a fact and a no-brainer.

Does this mean that you change your eligibility criteria for loyalty membership to become more inclusive? Not unless it is part of a deliberate strategy.

What it does mean is that you need to measure loyalty program effectiveness in ways that will minimise the self-selection bias. No – it cannot be eliminated altogether!

Let's look at metrics and measurement from two angles:

1. **Loyalty Program Performance**
2. **Loyalty Program Effectiveness**

The first is to look at the program in isolation and see how it is performing. The second is more nuanced and looks at how effective the program has been in impacting behaviour.

LOYALTY PROGRAM PERFORMANCE

This is the practice of looking at the program in isolation and tracking its performance. And what would "performance" mean? It depends on the objectives and deliverables that were stated at the outset for the program – and measurement of program performance against these.

In general, however, when you are looking at program performance, here is a set of questions you would ask yourself:

1. MEMBER BASE SIZE AND SCALE

    - Has my program attracted members and is the member base growing?

    - What % of total sales (revenue) is coming from my program?

    - Data cleanliness, population and standardisation rates

2. MEMBER BASE METRICS

- What are my member base metrics – Repeat rate, Repeat duration (inter-purchase period), Frequency, Average Transaction Value, Range, Total Value per year, New product/SKU trial rate?

- What is the member base retention rate? Point to note – REPEAT RATE refers to % members repeating visits within a specified period like a year. RETENTION RATE refers to % members who repeat ACROSS specified periods like a year – and are hence RETAINED across years

- An inverse of the above – what is the member base churn rate?

3. TIER PERFORMANCE

- What are member metrics by tier? (If your program has tiers)

- What are tier upgrades, downgrades, tier retention statistics?

4. ACCRUAL AND REDEMPTION

- What is the average, min, max currency earn – overall and by tier? (If your program has currency)

- What is the redemption rate? What % of members have redeemed (ever), what % of currency has been redeemed?

- What % of currency has expired? (Breakage %)

- What is the frequency of redemption? Average, min, max

- What is the pattern of redemption? Seasonality, popular items, no-redemption items

These are the broad quantitative/data-led metrics. But let it never be said that program performance is only about the numbers. There is a whole area of qualitative and softer metrics which are equally important – and, in fact, more important than quantitative metrics in the early years of the program.

Here are a few critical qualitative metrics that need to be tracked:

1. PROGRAM AWARENESS AND KNOWLEDGE

   - What % of members are aware that they are program members
   - What is the awareness of program features and benefits?
   - What is the awareness of their own status in the program? Tier, currency accumulated etc

2. PROGRAM PERCEPTION

   - Program Satisfaction levels
   - Net Promoter Score – a very important metric and designed to measure a higher level of loyalty than CS scores
   - Program referral rates and word of mouth
   - Expectations from the program
   - Program benchmarking against other programs they are members of

3. PROGRAM PARTICIPATION AND ENGAGEMENT

   - Participation in campaigns, promotions
   - Response to offers
   - Program White mail (unsolicited mail)
   - Program complaints
   - Program social media participation – visits, likes, shares, posts
   - Program event (online and offline) registration and attendance

SATISFACTION AND NET PROMOTER SCORE

A deeper look at the importance of measuring satisfaction - and why the Net Promoter Score is a higher measure of loyalty.

Why is it important to measure SATISFACTION?

- So you know what's going right and what's going wrong

- So you know where you stand w.r.t your competition

- So you know why you got the results you did – whether they were good or bad

- So you can act on what you learn from your members and forge stronger relationships…

The manifold pay-offs of keeping your member satisfied:

- The Members tell you what they want – and how they want it

- You tailor your product, service, loyalty program – to their wants

- The more the customer invests, the more is HIS/HER STAKE in making the relationship work

- He/She now finds it more convenient to remain with you than RE-TEACH a competitor

When measuring satisfaction, remember to keep two factors in mind:

- The IMPORTANCE of the attribute in the members' minds

- The SATISFACTION level of the members vs that attribute.

Let us now structure the attributes on IMPORTANCE VS SATISFACTION and define action points basis this:

In each of the quadrants you would place attributes that are measured – e.g. Program Enrolment Process, Program Currency, Program Rewards, Program Newsletter, Program Events, Program Tier upgrades and downgrades etc.

In terms of action, clearly the priority needs to be on attributes that are HIGH on importance and LOW on satisfaction. This is what needs immediate action. However, it is equally important to focus on attributes that are High on both Importance and Satisfaction.

This brings us to the next question: Is satisfaction enough?

Merely satisfied customers can be switched by your competition. What you need are completely satisfied customers who are then LOYAL to you. Asking about satisfaction is good….. But not enough. Satisfaction does not necessarily translate into reduced churn (60-80% of lost customers surveyed claimed they were 'satisfied' with the brand). Satisfaction does not necessarily translate into business growth.

So, we have a more evolved measure – **The Net Promoter Score**. The likelihood of a customer recommending your brand/ program is a predictive measure of loyalty. **Fred Reichheld**, the pioneer of NPS, wrote the book THE ULTIMATE QUESTION – where he propounded that there was one question that would be the closest measure of Loyalty. It was the very simple, very basic question – How likely are you to recommend us to your friend?

This question is based on the simple human truth that when customers act as references, they are putting their own reputation on the line. They typically take that risk only when they themselves are intensely loyal to you. They make a referral because they BELIEVE that they are getting superior value and they FEEL GOOD about the relationship they have.

Loyal customers show 4 kinds of behaviour:

- They come back for more
- They increase their purchases
- They refer their friends
- They invest their precious time for free

The Net Promoter Score operates on a ten-point scale when answering the question HOW LIKELY ARE YOU TO RECOMMEND US TO A FRIEND?

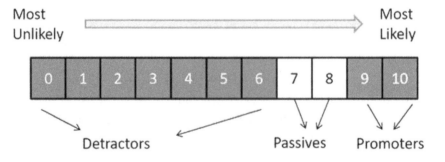

The significance of this measure is that it is – **simple, severe and sensitive**. Simple - It is one question. Severe because only ratings of 9 and 10 are considered PROMOTERS. And Sensitive because you are measuring it as **NET PROMOTER SCORE = % PROMOTERS (-) % DETRACTORS.**

The three clusters that emerge are:

- The Promoters – True advocates with highest rates of repurchase and referral

- The Passives – passively satisfied but probably stay due to inertia – a dangerous thing!

- The Detractors – who quickly spread negative word-of-mouth and lead to a drag on growth.

The task of every brand/ program is to figure out how to grow the promoters, minimise the detractors and elevate the passives into committed promoters.

MEASURING PROGRAM PERFORMANCE

Program Performance measurement needs to be holistic and timely. Measurement methods will be a combination of:

1. Program Data output and analysis – which will provide answers to all the hard metrics and some of the soft metrics as well. Monthly MIS reports on all the key hard metrics are a good way to track program performance regularly. It is also important to drill down into monthly MIS reports to arrive at conclusions at an overall level and also by market/zone, by kind of outlet, offline vs online and other relevant splits as per the business.

2. Program data will also give us the monthly performance measures on participation and response levels – including social media metrics.

3. Program Member research for the qualitative metrics like awareness, perception and attitudes. Ideally the research needs to be done half-yearly across a sample of members from all segments/tiers. For a new program you would start with research to set a baseline, and then repeat half yearly to track progress.

4. Content analysis of all program mail and complaints at member service centres. Monthly analysis and reporting.

At a broad level, program operating reports can be categorised as:

Transactional	Participation	Financial
Spend	Enrollment quantity & source	Program liability
Frequency	Redemptions	Point distribution
Tender	Web & social metrics	Event liability
Location/channel	Call center	Program budget to actual
Merchant	E-mail	Event budget to actual
SKU	Offer response & qualification	

More sophisticated loyalty programs will organise and view Operational Reports as:

1. Based on Segments

2. Distribution vs basic statistical measures of Mean, Median, Mode

3. Discrete vs Continuous time periods

4. Change vs previous period

Both REPORTING and ANALYSIS are equally important. Reporting is a statement of FACT as the data shows. ANALYSIS has a predictive view.

A report will tell you what % of loyalty program members have not transacted in X period of time. Analysis will predict what is the probability of members churning within the next time period.

Reports will tell you WHO responded to WHAT offer. Analysis will tell you who is LIKELY TO RESPOND to a particular offer.

And the importance of ANALYSIS takes us to the next aspect of Loyalty Program Measurement.

LOYALTY PROGRAM EFFECTIVENESS

Let us now look at the second aspect of program measurement. Loyalty Program Effectiveness. This will answer the question "Has my program impacted behaviour?"

This will attempt to address the issue of self-selection bias that we spoke about earlier. Has the program really impacted behaviour or is it just that my members are my more valuable customers and hence doing better on all metrics?

One can never eliminate self-selection bias altogether. But there is a range of methods one can use to measure loyalty program IMPACT or EFFECTIVENESS, from MOST DEFENSIBLE to LEAST DEFENSIBLE

Ideal Loyalty Measurement (most defensible)				Secondary Measurement Options (faster / easier to execute)		
Hold-Out Control Group vs. Members*	Control Market vs. Program Market*	**Create Quasi-Control Group (Post-Launch)***	Participator vs.Non-Participators	Pre vs. Post Behavior Shifts (Members Only)	Members vs. Non-Members (No pre-post analysis)

1. The ideal measurement of effectiveness is to have a hold-out matched control group from amongst members, which does not receive program communication, offers etc. This control group is selected prior to program campaigns. This is the cleanest comparison possible as it controls for all potential differences in behaviour. However, in today's day of instant and social media, it is very difficult to isolate the control group completely from exposure to all program communication. So you will have members of the control group migrating to the test group without being identified – and this will skew results.

2. Control market – this becomes relevant only when the program is not prevalent nationally. Important to select a control market that is identical – or at least very similar in characteristics to the program market/s – and that is a big problem in itself. Every

market may also have local, unexpected in-market events which will skew results

3. Creating Quasi Control groups – Paired Comparison – A matched group of non-members is selected after the campaign/ program with the goal of matching the test group based on their profile prior to launch. Pre vs. post is examined for both quasi-control group & members in the program. This is still susceptible to the responder bias argument though the effect may have been minimized to some extent.

4. Participator vs Non-Participator - Selected from within the member base, this measures the impact of program engagement (participation, redemption, multiple redemption) within the program member base. Most often this just compares current (post) metrics. The concept is that members who are more engaged with the program will display more valuable behaviour. This is however also susceptible to the chicken-egg syndrome. Valuable members get more value from the program and hence participate more.

5. Pre vs Post Behaviour shifts of only members. The concept here is that the program would have positively impacted member behaviour such that their metrics will improve significantly vs where they were pre-program. Essentially if they were showing a certain growth pre-program, has the growth incrementally improved post program membership? Has the SLOPE of the graph showing the trend become steeper post membership?

6. Member vs Non-Member analysis - this is the most commonly used method across most programs to measure program effectiveness. But the least defensible when it comes to self-selection bias.

While we find that no method of measurement is immune to self-selection bias, a combination of methods used can give a reasonably good view of program impact and effectiveness.

To repeat, the basic principles of program measurement are: Measuring the RIGHT VARIABLES at the RIGHT TIME by the RIGHT METHODS.

Goes back to commonsense. It's not that hard!

CHAPTER 16

GETTING LOYALTY OFF THE GROUND

"It's supposed to be hard. If it was easy, everybody would do it!"
Tom Hanks "A League of Their Own"

Someone once said, "A goal without a plan is just a WISH!" You can have the best strategy, the most appropriate design – if you don't have a plan of action to get it off the ground, your design will remain on paper and never see the light of day.

The key to a good implementation plan is to, first and foremost, provide for CONTINGENCIES. Remember your entire design is based on assumptions of what is likely to happen. No one is a soothsayer. The assumptions were made based on reason and logic backed by whatever data was available – but the proof of the pudding is in the eating. You will actually know what has happened once you execute. And results may be below or above what you predicted – so you must be prepared for that as well.

SEQUENCE OF ACTION

Once the design is approved internally, and the financial model is also given the go-ahead, here are some of the next steps :

- **CONCEPT TESTING AND BASELINE RESEARCH**

  This is said with immense caution. You have already taken the decision to go ahead, you have already done enough research to support the fact that you need a loyalty initiative and what form it should take. The stage of Concept Testing is just to ratify the final design with proposition and pillars - and fine-tune any details if required. This is not a go-no go decision on Loyalty itself.

  Concept testing can be combined with PRE-PROGRAM research to set baseline benchmarks against which program performance will be measured.

- **PROGRAM RULE BOOK**

  The Program Design is converted into a detailed Program Rule Book which will list every single program decision, the rule options evaluated, and the rationale for the final decision taken. For e.g. Eligibility – what were the options evaluated and what was the final decision taken and why. There are at least 100-120 program decisions that need to be outlined in the Program Rule Book.

- **BRANDING OF PROGRAM AND PROGRAM PROPERTIES**

  It is best to get your mainline agency to work on the program branding as well. Branding elements will include: program brand name, logo and tagline, website design, app design (as applicable), branding guidelines and style manual in terms of look and feel of communication elements

- **COMMUNICATION AND ACTIVITY PLAN**

  Work out a detailed communication and activity plan – by segment – for the program – for the first year. We have discussed the format of this earlier in the book. Decisions are to be taken on segments, communication elements, messaging, channel, frequency and scheduling. The plan will include program activities and events as well.

- MEMBER SERVICES SUPPORT

This involves a study of existing customer support services that are available – and whether they can be leveraged for member support. Remember that program queries and grievances are different from general brand queries and complaints, and will need devoted resources. Decisions are then to be taken on the type of member support – call centre, web support, chat agents/ bots etc. The plan will cover resources required, timing of member support (normally need not be 24x7), capability, hardware and infrastructure, member service software, member FAQs and their answers all mapped out – and agent training. A member service and support manual will specify the TATs, escalation matrix for query resolution, exception reporting, process mapping and reporting formats.

- EMPLOYEE ORIENTATION

Relevant departments within the Organisation need to be oriented on the program offering and the impact of the same on their respective roles. This will follow a systematic process of tailored presentations to each department with supporting documents giving the program details. Customer facing employees need to be given intensive training on program features and benefits, member FAQs and query resolution. Levels of empowerment for issue resolution need to be defined clearly.

- PROGRAM PROCESS MAPPING

Who says loyalty program design is not about detail! Every single process involved in the program, post completion of design, needs to be clearly mapped out in a process map. Technology is not involved as yet. This is just a mapping of the process to be followed when each event happens - Trace a member's journey through the program and you will get an idea of processes to be mapped - to whit a few:

- Eligibility decision
- Enrolment
- Member welcome - message and fulfilment if any
- Member transaction tracking
- Profile updation
- Member earn
- Member burn
- Points reconciliation
- Rewards catalogue updation
- Redemption fulfilment
- Member complaints
- Member queries
- Member referral
- Tier upgrade
- Tier downgrade
- Membership validity
- Membership renewal
- Social media tracking
- Member milestone achievement

- **PROGRAM TECHNOLOGY**

This is the biggest step in implementation and will take the longest time. Even the simplest program design will require some technology for execution. While there are several options for technology, and several service providers who will take over from here, here are some logical steps to follow when planning for technology:

- The program design is converted into a Technical Specifications Document – the Program Rule Book is the feeder document for the Tech Specs document.

- The mapped processes are compiled in a process manual

- Audit of existing technology and infrastructure available in-house, for marketing communications - and system specifications for the same

- Evaluate system requirements – typically a combination of these is required – loyalty engine, analytics engine, marketing communications platform, redemption platform, API integration for app and website as applicable, API integration with partners for partner programs, mobile app

- Evaluate alternate tech providers in terms of specialisation and ability to meet one or more of the system requirements. Criteria for evaluation would be: Credibility and reputation of the provider, scope of offering, pricing range, training and orientation support, after-sales support, hardware that will seamlessly integrate with existing systems and infrastructure with minimal dissonance, final performance of entire system with least friction for the member, and most importantly, timelines to go live. A decision may be taken to go with multiple providers, each with their own specialisation, as long as the systems are able to talk to each other

- Discussion with tech provider/s on alternate business and commercial model arrangements. Options considered are – end-to-end outsourcing with single point of contact, in-house operation with some support from the provider, SAAS (software as a service) models, Build-Operate-Transfer (BOT) models

- **PROGRAM LAUNCH**

Give the program the best chance of success by launching it well. Have a well-planned launch that covers internal orientation, on-field orientation that builds up to an internal launch event, and a Go-Live event with customers. The biggest enrolment surge happens at launch, so use the opportunity to create enough awareness of the program and its benefits. The importance of Point-of-Sale material and presence in mass media as tag-ons to brand advertising, cannot be over emphasised. Keep aside a portion of the budget to launch the program with some noise – most often this is compromised and then you're already on the back-foot before the program is even in the market.

- **HR METRICS**

If the program is to be taken seriously internally and given enough weight and importance, it is vital to integrate program KPIs to HR performance evaluation cycles. As an example, when the program is launched, enrolment is a KPI that needs to be built-in to all staff responsible for enrolment – Store Managers for instance. Similarly, as the program gains traction, member transaction metrics will be a KPI for marketing. Member query resolution will be a KPI for the Call centre. And likewise. That is the only way Loyalty permeates through the organisation and begins to positively impact all functions and disciplines.

- **ORGANISATION STRUCTURE FOR LOYALTY**

This brings us to the final point. It is worth thinking deeply about how the program is going to evolve and what sort of Organisation structure is required to support it. While it will invariably start with being the responsibility of Marketing, as it evolves and begins to monetise itself, there is a viable option to spin it off as a separate business unit with its own Organisation structure. This takes time, vision and commitment. But even within marketing, it is useful to assign key responsibilities specific to loyalty to sub-functions

– loyalty communications, loyalty analytics, program operations, partnerships, program strategy etc. While there may be outsourced service providers to handle some of these, it is always necessary to allocate responsibility within the marketing team, for better control and oversight.

When you get into loyalty, remember that it is a marathon and not a sprint. Plan for it carefully – it will evolve seamlessly. It's not that hard!

CHAPTER 17

INDIA'S LOYALTY LANDSCAPE

TRENDS AND PRACTICES

"[India is] the One land that all men desire to see, and having seen once, by even a glimpse, would not give that glimpse for all the shows of all the rest of the globe combined." – *Mark Twain*

Much has been spoken about the size, scale and diversity that India offers. It is not just the huge potential our country offers – it is also about the leaps we have made over the past decade leaving most economies behind.

India offers a unique blend of tradition and modernity. Arguably the greatest intellectual talent – and paradoxically, the cheapest workforce.

Let's look at some of the projected numbers:

1. 1 in 2 Households to be Upper Middle and High Income by 2030

2. Domestic consumption predicted to be USD 6 Trn by 2030

3. 1 Billion internet users by 2030

Mind boggling to say the least!

And the Indian Household Income profile – projected to move from a traditional pyramid structure to a bloated middle.

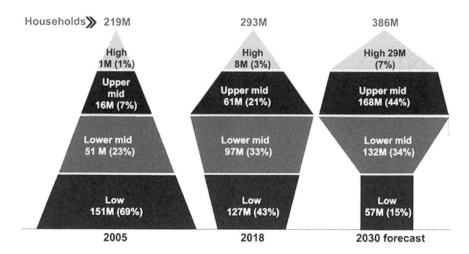

Source : Bain World Economic Forum Report 2019

And the drivers of future consumption in India?

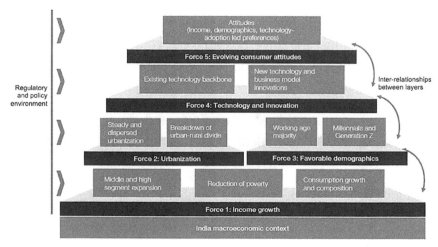

We will see an India that is RICHER, YOUNGER, MORE CONFIDENT, MORE CONNECTED – and every one of these factors will influence Loyalty Marketing.

THE INDIAN LEAPFROG

As we see the West moving through stages of development, we seem to have learned through observation and have almost leapfrogged to the future. While the intermediate stages do exist, there are many who have jumped several steps ahead into the future.

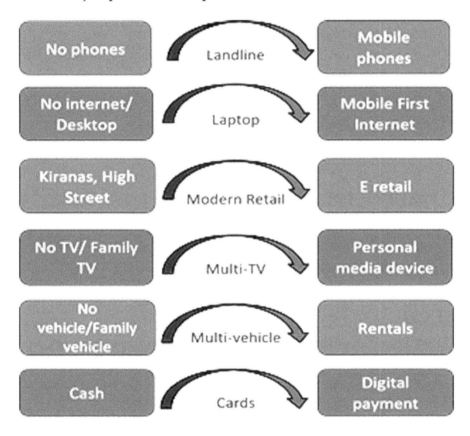

Three surrogate indicators for loyalty in India:

1. Steady increase in Credit Card issuance – although the reward giveback is declining across banks

2. Mobile wallets – multiple options – all growing

3. And UPI transactions – exploding in Value and Volume.

Out of the total 51.91 billion UPI transactions conducted between January and June 2023, 29.15 billion were P2M (Person to Merchant) payments, accounting for approximately 56.1% of the total. The United Payments Interface (UPI) transactions in India surged by 62% in the first half of 2023 when compared to the same period last year.

Programs like Zillion (erstwhile Payback), Reliance One and Flipkart SuperCoins have over 100 million registered members each – and there are others like Shoppers Stop First Citizen, Amazon Prime, Starbucks Rewards who have memberships in the 10-20 million range.

A spokesperson for the recent Tata Neu program said in 2022: "The journey of Tata Neu has begun with a cumulative consumer base of 120 million users, 2,500 offline stores, along with an 80 million app footprint across our digital assets,"

The scale of programs is unimaginable across the board.

LOYALTY TRENDS AND PRACTICES ACROSS VERTICALS

A quick overview of the key trends and practices we are seeing in Loyalty across verticals in India.

RETAIL

Under this category we consider all types of retail – grocery, department store, specialty retail, hypermarkets, single-brand retail, QSRs

Retail Loyalty is characterised by high fragmentation. There are multiple programs running, with small member bases. Individual brands often tend to launch their own programs due to competitive pressure, with little more than currency or discounts as an offering.

Retail brands mostly start off as individual programs (Proprietary) and then move on to Partnership models with partners adding to the value proposition with either licensing of program currency or with targeted offers to the program member base.

The core proposition for most retail programs in India centres around program currency (points when you shop) and/or discounts for program members. Apart from a limited component of Priority Offering (Access to events, member sales, member shopping hours etc) there is little differential treatment in-store. Most brands do not yet have the technology to RECOGNISE a program member (and the tier) as he/she walks-in to the store. Identification of membership is most often at the check-out counter - hence differential experience whilst shopping is not always an offering.

With the additional logistic challenges of having a separate check-out counter for program members or top tier members, or separate trial rooms (for apparel retail), the difficulty lies in creating suitably differentiated value propositions.

Special mentions need to be made of programs like Shoppers Stop First Citizen launched in 1994, still going strong, constantly evolving in structure and offering and accounting to close to 90% of the brand's total sales. IKEA Family, more recently launched (along with the brand's entry into India in Hyderabad in 2018) offers a strongly differentiated proposition based not on currency but on special member pricing and communication that reflects the innovativeness of the parent brand. MyStarbucks Rewards is a gold standard in loyalty programs globally and features strongly in India as well, with the entire program being driven through the app.

ECOMMERCE

Given the digital boom that India is seeing, Ecommerce programs are first and foremost characterised by extremely large members bases. Programs are "inclusive" in that SHOPPER = MEMBER because of the ability to track at a single customer level for ecommerce.

Propositions have a currency and/or discounts – and you also have an elevated service offering for a paid membership as with Amazon Prime.

Discounts are a hygiene part of Ecommerce propositions – whether or not it is a "program" offering - and a key driver offering for customers to shop online in India is better prices.

Apart from transactional rewards (with currency and discounts), there is some element of differentiation through service and privilege elements – free delivery, delivery in 24 hours, early access to sales, priority access to merchandise etc. The challenge lies in going beyond that and creating differentiated experiences.

Special mentions of – Amazon Prime – which has a large and committed member base with high renewal rates. A very large part of the offering here is Prime Video which is driving the stickiness.

Flipkart SuperCoins – large and almost ubiquitous, as the currency is being actively externalised.

Nykaa, the beauty platform, recently launched Nykaa Prive~ - a multi-tiered program - centred around points based on value of purchase and some benefits. An innovative angle introduced is points for product reviews. The jury is out on how the program is performing.

TRAVEL AND HOSPITALITY

We discuss Airline and Hotel programs in this category.

The Airline industry saw a fair amount of turbulence with the massive collapse of Jet Airways and Go Air also threatening to go under.

The Jet Privilege program had always been a marquee loyalty program (as big and known as the parent brand Jet Airways) with best practice components of currency, benefits, services and privileges. Launched as proprietary, it soon evolved into a strong partner ecosystem. With the collapse of Jet, the program in isolation continued to have a good valuation and has since become InterMiles. With the absence of the single anchor partner – Jet Airways – the program has however lost much of its sheen.

Air India's Flying Returns (now part of Tata Neu), Club Vistara (also soon to be part of Tata Neu) are the other significant programs in the airline space in India. All programs follow the traditional global principles of currency earn (based on a combination of haul and fare), tiered structure, tangible benefits (separate check-in counters, priority baggage, priority boarding etc) and privileges like lounge access. They are all also partner programs with synergistic partners tied in.

Hotel programs in India are also characterised by strong and relevant partnerships especially in adjacent categories – airlines, car rentals for e.g. Propositions centre around points, recognition and special services. Free nights against points is a huge draw. And special treatment and experiences in-property is a huge motivator as well – be it a welcome drink, complimentary breakfast, a room upgrade, access to the business centre, complimentary spa treatment or a free airport pick up.

Hotels also sometimes have frequent dining programs independent of the stay programs. Dining programs are most often fee based and they offer subsequent discounts on dining along with the main program currency. Taj Epicure is an example.

Mentions to be made of Taj Inner Circle (now part of Tata Neu), Marriott Bonvoy (program is as big as the parent brand), Club ITC (exists on its own as well as being part of Marriott Bonvoy) and, more recently, Oberoi One.

BANKING AND FINANCIAL SERVICES (BFSI)

Characterised by a plethora of credit card programs – bank cards as well as co-branded credit cards with retail, travel, hospitality, e-commerce platforms, fuel. Private label credit cards which are white-labelled by banks, are not yet as predominant in India as in the West, where many retail chains have their own credit cards.

We are also beginning to see bank-wide programs (e.g. ICICI bank) which reward and recognize customers for stickiness across bank products and services. Since this is dependent on a single customer view across the bank and is controlled centrally, hopefully we will see less of the communication overload we experience with each bank product – home loans, personal loans, debit cards, travel cards, forex etc - operating in a silo. Given the widely differential margins across all bank products, giveback in the form of currency will also vary widely.

Most card programs offer a currency – the value of which has been steadily going down over the past few years due to affordability becoming more and more stringent. Currency is redeemable against a catalogue that is periodically refreshed.

The catalogues typically have a range of rewards across popular categories like appliances, electronics, technology etc. What we have also seen in recent years is the predominance of vouchers which makes fulfilment a much easier task. Vouchers of e-commerce platforms are a popular redemption item.

Charity makes a presence in almost all bank catalogues with several NGOs giving members an opportunity to redeem their points for donations to their preferred charity.

Most card programs operate in the background and are not actively promoted or pushed. The exception is American Express, whose Membership Rewards program is a strong property and is prominent in all the brand communication.

Card programs are, in fact, often financially modelled for breakage - assuming low redemption rates. Not a healthy outcome for loyalty. They are also banking (pun intended!) on the fact that, by nature, financial institutions have stickiness and customers find it difficult to exit once they become customers.

The challenge for BFSI loyalty is to infuse more innovation and customer orientation to their loyalty initiatives and make them more experiential vs transactional.

FUEL AND TELECOM/OTT

Very different verticals in nature but grouped together here because they both operate in a high frequency, low margin environment. Telecom and fuel both have a very strong presence in loyalty globally because they are frequency drivers.

Fuel in India is by and large Govt controlled with three major players – HPCL, BPCL and IOCL. We are now seeing the entry of private players like Shell, Reliance/ Jio BP and Nayara. Fuel itself operates on a low to almost negative margin so, while we have loyalty programs across almost all the players, the giveback is minuscule. Some fuel players operate on a dual model where they have their own programs but are also part of the large coalitions where total member earnings accrue across partners/sponsors and then become meaningful to the member.

Giveback is higher for convenience stores at fuel pumps, for lubricants and for auto services offered at the pumps.

Fuel loyalty is unfortunately constrained by the affordability – partnerships and coalitions may be the way out.

Telecom/OTT players in India have not made any significant dent in the loyalty landscape as yet despite the huge opportunity. They can track every customer, they know the exact details of every customer's usage habits and they have a plethora of voice, data and other value-added services to offer – it should have been a loyalty playground! The problem in India is that many players are still trying to make themselves financially viable before venturing into loyalty.

What we do see in telecom is premium priced "service packages" and offer booklets that comprise offers from a multitude of partners that are generically circulated amongst members – all of which may have been negotiated well but most of which are barely relevant! There is also an overload of irrelevant communication that goes out.

The challenge for telecom loyalty is basic – establish a presence in loyalty – either alone or with partners. Drive relevance.

FOOD TECH/MOBILITY TECH

We cannot have a discussion on verticals without speaking of the new-age industry entrants of food tech and mobility tech. Or, in other words – Swiggy/Zomato and Ola/Uber – all of which have become generic names for their respective categories!

Each of these players boast of 100-200 mn customers on record with at least 1-2 mn of them subscribing to their premium offerings – Swiggy One, Zomato Gold, Ola Select, Uber Premium. These are their paid loyalty initiatives.

Premium offerings in these categories are paid subscriptions and come with elevated service levels and benefits - better pricing, priority bookings, quicker delivery, free delivery, better cars, better drivers etc, etc.

All 4 of these players operate off apps which have integrated payment wallets as well. They have started building services around the core proposition (food delivery, rides) for better asset utilisation (cars and delivery agents) – and ultimately driving greater stickiness with their customers/members.

Food tech and mobility tech would do well to structure themselves around a free plus paid loyalty model, where the large base that has NOT subscribed to the paid offering also has reason to stick to one brand. Right now, for most of us, the names and offerings are both frequently interchangeable! Uber-Ola often becomes Ula-Ober – such is the duplication in our minds!

COALITIONS

A discussion on verticals must logically end with a loyalty program model that is across verticals – the Coalition.

Very prominent in Europe and Canada (Air Miles, Nectar being examples), coalitions did not take off the way they were expected to in the US.

In India, Coalitions are making their presence felt in various formats. Since we have large business conglomerates in India which straddle different verticals, CLOSED COALITIONS (that we spoke of earlier) exist and flourish. Reliance One is a prominent example, with a claimed membership base of 200 million plus members. Titan Industries had their own coalition – Titan Encircle – which has now become part of Tata Neu. And yes, Tata Neu- the latest in the fold - with an exhaustive and enviable set of Tata brands, and a huge existing customer base within its fold.

In the Open Coalition format, we have Zillion – erstwhile Payback – which also speaks of 100 mn plus members, and has sponsors/partners across most verticals.

Since there is also a plethora of small independent brands in India – who may not have the wherewithal to run their own program – coalitions become an optimum solution for them to make an entry into loyalty.

LOYALTY TRENDS AND PRACTICES – INDIA VS INTERNATIONAL

A study of the loyalty landscape in India must logically end with understanding what makes India special and different from global markets and what are the implications for loyalty marketing in India.

- **AUDIENCE**

  When one speaks of India, most often the first word that comes to mind is DIVERSITY. While you may see homogeneous and distinct audience clusters globally, in India one is faced with a heterogeneous audience with diverse income, exposure, attitudes – and language. This may well imply that a one-size-fits-all program may not be applicable for a nationwide loyalty initiative in India. You may well need variants to suit the audience being catered to.

- **VALUE PROPOSITION**

  As yet, most program propositions in India focus around hard rewards and tangibility. The softer aspects are making their presence felt, but not significantly enough. We are leaps ahead in technology to be able to deliver any proposition that we think of – and yet, something like gamification is still very, very nascent as a part of loyalty. Creating a balanced and more holistic proposition will be the way to go

- **TECHNOLOGY**

  We have a dichotomy here. We have advanced technology; we have leapfrogged to digital versions for most programs - and yet we still have an audience that may well need the physical format of the program – card and all. We often find that technology tends to dictate program design, when it actually needs to be the other way around, given that we have the capability to deliver to any design, any proposition.

- **PAYMENT INTEGRATION**

  Where we see private label cards dictated by the brand, and backed by the bank, prominent in loyalty in US and Europe, India has not seen much of a presence of private label payment instruments. What you see are co-branded program cards dictated by banks – and that is likely to continue in the near future as well. What we also see is payment wallets integrated with apps, and programs rewarding use of specific payment instruments (specific cards, UPI wallets).

- **SOCIAL CAUSE INTEGRATION**

  Well-integrated for most evolved brands in the West, in India social cause and larger purpose is limited but has made an entry. With most programs being targeted at Gen Y, Gen Z and Gen Alpha – this is likely to become a crucial program differentiator.

- **METRICS AND FINANCIALS**

  Loyalty being more evolved in the West, we see the use of nuanced metrics and analytics to evaluate effectiveness of programs. Indian programs still largely stick to topline metrics of base, growth, activity and transaction metrics. We are likely to see more and more of predictive analytics, CLTV calculation-based strategies emerging.

- **ORGANISATION STRUCTURE**

  Loyalty most often sits within Marketing in Indian organisations. Evolved programs globally may have a separate loyalty team directly under C Suite purview because loyalty is meant to impact the whole Enterprise and not just marketing. This is still to make a presence in India.

- **EMPLOYEE EMPOWERMENT**

  Limited but improving in India. To bring softer benefits to life on the ground, it will become critical to train customer-facing employees on program features and benefits and differentiated treatment of members. It will also become important to empower them to address and resolve program queries and complaints on the floor as and when raised. This will include the power to award benefits, bonuses, surprises etc on the spot.

- **STATE OF INDUSTRY**

    And, finally, lots to look forward to in Loyalty in India. Sunrise industry still, growing rapidly – opportunity looms large.

Designing for loyalty initiatives in India will require a grasp of the loyalty landscape we are operating in – and the developments we are likely to see in the future.

Surely - "There's no place like home" *Wizard of Oz*

CHAPTER 18

LOYALTY 2023 AND BEYOND

"The time has come," the Walrus said, "To talk of many things: Of shoes — and ships — and sealing-wax — Of cabbages — and kings — And why the sea is boiling hot — And whether pigs have wings." The Walrus and the Carpenter, Lewis Carroll

There is a lot going for Loyalty in the years ahead. Optimism is ripe, the environment is conducive, the need is real and urgent and the attitude is positive, yet demanding.

We are faced with a growing Gen Y, Gen Z and Gen Alpha, who are going to be the target audience for most initiatives from brands – and whose requirements and expectations are clear. Loyalty means something very different – and very specific to them.

Technology has shown quantum leaps – the Segment of One is real and implementable. Real-time, on-the-fly execution is the norm. Batch processing? Archaic!

Gone are the days when you could believe that tying the customer down to a time-based 'contract' is loyalty. Today it is about freedom, choice and control with the customer. *Set them free and they will come back* – is the adage to go by.

Loyalty is much more than a plan, more than a strategy. It is a philosophy and needs to be driven top-down and executed bottom-up in an organisation if it is to flourish.

As we come to the end of our loyalty journey, let us take a deep-dive into some of the trends that we are likely to see in the years to come.

Here are some aspects that are already there – and will only get enhanced further:

- **Ultra-personalisation** – technology makes it quite easily possible to address a segment of 1. It will therefore be possible to literally speak to each member based on their personal and transaction history and profile with relevant messaging. And this is going to become the norm. If not segment of one, micro-segmentation will be the way to go. No more will all members of the Platinum tier get the same messaging. The traditional tiering as we know it, will continue to be a part of program structure and external manifestation of status – but ultra-personalisation will lead to a completely new level of differentiation made possible by technology.

- **Seamless omni-channel delivery** – this is hygiene now. Initiatives are expected to play across mediums, and seamlessly recognise the customer/member through whichever medium they choose to interact in. And this includes social media. More and more will you see social media reactions and feedback, being integrated with program initiatives. The choice of channel is with the member – though you may choose to differentially reward use of one channel vs another as a program deliverable. This will include app and website play for all programs – and the effort to differentiate and value-add to each of these channels of delivery, so that it is truly meaningful to the member. The key to remember – don't have multiple channels just for the sake of having them. Each channel of interaction must add value to the member. Each channel must recognise member interactions across all other channels that are available and communicate accordingly. And needless to say, each channel must recognise who the member is without seeking repeated login information!

- **Data-driven decision making** – A no-brainer. Already there, and it is only going to get enhanced. All communication will be based on insights from data available. Relevance will be the key program differentiator. The development we are likely to see is the use of multiple kinds of data to arrive at a holistic view of the customer – profile data, transaction/behaviour data, social media data, research data overlaid (attitudes and perceptions), customer care centre data, spontaneous/white mail - and finally syndicated data available on geography, population, demographics, other statistics. As we see more and more of multiple kinds of data overlaid, it builds a more well-rounded view of the member and his/her motivations and expectations – leading to more meaningful segmentation, and more relevant messaging. Remember, when digital is the primary delivery mode, you are largely playing with short messages (often 160 characters!) – the quicker you build the connect and drive relevance, the more positive the outcome will be.

- **Building emotional connect** – We have discussed repeatedly that hard benefits are almost hygiene in a program proposition and can easily be replicated. What makes the brand different, special, closer to the member, is the emotional connect. Programs will consciously build value propositions that focus heavily on the emotion – the softer benefits, the larger purpose, the feel-good privileges, the ultra-personalised service – all of which will create stickiness and retention much more than hard benefits ever can. Emotional connect initiatives will rely heavily on data for insights into the member.

- **Experiential offerings** – Gen Y, Gen Z and Gen Alpha put a price on experiences much more than "goods". This will become an important pillar in most program propositions.

Experiential offerings tailor-made to the program purpose and resonating with the audience will be key. As a simple example, social cause will be about much more than donating to your favourite charity. It will be about creating an experience for you as donor and giving an experience to the beneficiary where the donor feels that he/she has consciously used time well and made a tangible difference. Holiday rewards may be less about the tried and tested and more about the experimental and innovative – See the 7 Wonders of the World vs a generic trip to Europe. It will be about creating talking points, that then go viral and create positive word-of-mouth for the program. It does not matter if only a few members become eligible for the offering - the news value and virality it will result in will rub-off on the entire member base and create desirability amongst non-members.

- **User-Generated Content** – or, for loyalty, member-generated content. This refers to content generated by users – reviews, photos, videos – that showcase their experience with the brand/program. In a world of social media where influencer marketing is gaining so much traction and so quickly, UGC will be the route to building credibility. Programs already have member panels to seek feedback, they have newsletters/e-zines where they showcase members and they have linkages to social media where members are asked to like/share/post pictures and videos. This is going to increase and is going to take new forms. We are going to see members actively contributing to communication content for the program – and this will be beyond product/brand usage and reviews. Programs which are smart will quickly begin to allow privileged customers to use the program as an avenue for their name and fame within the guardrails of the overall program proposition – and this is going to become a major weapon of stickiness for members.

- **Payment Instruments** – We are already beginning to see payment instruments being integrated with loyalty. What this really attempts to do is a double-change in behaviour – not only does the program incentivise you to buy (more, more often), it incentivises you further, to purchase using a specific payment instrument vs others. Loyalty programs in the West have been doing this for years. Private label cards of department stores (backed by banks) offer higher points when compared to using other payment instruments. Nordstrom's Nordy Club offers higher points on Nordstrom credit and debit cards. There are several programs that are entirely credit card based - Saks First, Neiman Marcus InCircle for e.g. Starbucks Rewards – a great example. The entire program operates through the app and the wallet that is in-built in the app. The scale of this program is so large, and the money sitting in the wallets is so high that Starbucks has been described as "A Bank that sells coffee!" Closer home, Tata Neu has a co-branded credit card with HDFC Bank which offers a substantially higher earn. What we will also begin to see is a plethora of offers linked to use of payment instruments. Big Basket shows you a range of offers at check-out – all linked to banks and usage of their cards. Chaayos is emulating Starbucks by promoting their own wallet and app. Payment instruments are being seen as a way to promote greater stickiness and entrenchment in the program. Financially and commercially, it makes sense for the program because the financial institution (the bank or the NBFC) is subsidising a part of the giveback, as they have much to gain as well. How easy it will be to drive a long-term habit change with a payment instrument is still to be seen. The jury is out.

And now let's specifically talk of trends we are going to see take front and centre stage in Loyalty over the next few years!

1. GAMIFICATION

Gamification has always been spoken of in connection with loyalty. What is Loyalty Marketing other than gamification? We are using tools and levers of reward and recognition to modify behaviour such that it is mutually rewarding. That is the essence of gamification.

And no, gamification does not mean introducing games into your loyalty program offering. It does not mean "play this game and you will earn points" - not unless the game is an integral part of the overall strategy.

At the core of Gamification lies the doctrine of INTRINSIC REINFORCEMENT. You challenge yourself, achieve your goals, get rewards and recognition. It so happens that your goals are your brand's goals as well. A loyalty marketing initiative that integrates gamification well, will ensure that it is a seamless part of the overall proposition where brand and program objectives are linked to reward and recognition. Remember that COERCED rewards - "Do this or else" or "If you don't do this, you don't get this" don't work as well as positive reinforcement.

The four tools that make gamification successful include:

- Competition - you achieve, you get rewards - you are competing with yourself and others

- Co-operation - you work together towards a common goal

- Instant Feedback - you know how you are performing, you get instant gratification, you are rewarded early and often

- Recognition - apart from rewards you are treated special, you are recognized, you are given status and privilege.

Loyalty initiatives that consciously incorporate these elements into their strategy will be able to build stronger member engagement.

Gamification will begin to be an integral part of reward strategy. Rewards may be extrinsic or intrinsic. Typically, intrinsic rewards are more motivating than extrinsic rewards. For a socially conscious audience for e.g. rewarding them with opportunities to volunteer for a good cause, facilitate learning interactions with social leaders etc will be a big driver.

However, programs will also need extrinsic rewards. And in order of most to least stickiness, these would be: **STATUS, ACCESS, POWER and STUFF.**

Status is the opportunity to openly or subtly brag to others while feeling good about what you have achieved. Status is also indicated by badges, tokens, leaderboards, seeing your name in public, personal fame through the program, listening to your feedback and acting on it.

Access is the ability to attain experiences and meet people – things that are curated and cannot be had for money. Brands will start leveraging their spokespersons in their loyalty initiatives – especially so if the spokesperson is a celebrity. Imagine a lunch with a cricketer or footballer. Access also refers to access to exclusive content – as desirable behaviour is demonstrated, more and more exclusive content is unlocked.

Power is the ability to share your joy and benefits with others – like inviting one friend along on a shopping spree, sharing your special member rate with someone, being allowed to bring a plus one to a member event.

And finally, **STUFF** – the rewards you would normally get against your currency. Things. Gifts. Surprises. Also good, easily scalable, and will be available to the entire member base contingent on behaviour.

Program initiatives will cover all four of these in various proportions. The Nike Run Club is a stellar example of gamification that is completely integrated with the product, the brand and the program. A completely free run-tracking and training app, it has no paid tier and offers alternate training plans. All the best practices of gamification are in play here – competing with yourself, tracking your performance against others, sharing your progress, getting counsel and advice, access to runs and other events, news and happenings – and yes, special rates on Nike footwear is the only "transactional" link with the brand. There is no currency, no accrual, no deals and offers beyond member rates. The content and gamification techniques are so engaging, this has become a best practice for emulation by others.

2. BRAND PURPOSE

Brand purpose is emerging as a key trend in many loyalty programs. Brand purpose is the brand (or company's) reason for being beyond profitability. That is what stays in the long run. Customers are increasingly drawn towards brands that are making a positive contribution – giving back to society, taking a stand on social and environmental issues – doing good in the world.

We have earlier discussed the importance of having a larger purpose to the program. This will soon become a need-to-have rather than an after-thought. Program strategic thinking will begin with a larger purpose that fits with the overall brand larger purpose. And the program proposition will stem from that, the pillars and offerings will link back to that in some fashion.

Sustainability, eco-friendly practices, good labour practices, renewable energy, waste reduction, gender and race equality, literacy, girl child, nutrition – brands are going to be called upon to take a stand on some or all of these – and programs will follow suit.

The trends of building emotional connect and stickiness will soon begin to hinge on linkages to larger purpose. We earlier spoke of Simon Sinek's Start with Why. Once that is in place, the How and What will follow easily – and will also be more meaningful and longer-term.

The H&M Program rewards customers for making sustainable loyalty choices. Members receive "Conscious points" every time they purchase items labelled as "Conscious". Conscious points can also be earned by recycling clothes in H&Ms Garment Collection program. Members who recycle receive tangible rewards.

Recyclebank US helps create a more sustainable future by rewarding people for taking **everyday green actions with discounts and deals** from local and national businesses. Recyclebank's mission is to motivate individuals and communities to realize a world in which nothing is wasted – changing how people view their role in creating a sustainable future. In order to catalyze these changes Recyclebank created a "currency" in the form of a rewards program that motivates, incentivises and rewards people to engage in "green" behaviours, like recycling and reducing energy usage, in a household setting.

Social purpose need not be boring. It can be fun – as Disney showed us. Disney had a dual objective of promoting VOLUNTEERISM and attendance at their theme parks. What did they do? Combined the two. The company partnered with American charitable and non-profit organizations to provide volunteer opportunities; individuals who volunteered with associated charities and non-profits received a voucher for one free admission to a Walt Disney World Resort or Disneyland Resort theme park. This was an excellent way of leveraging "Brand Disney" and it made volunteering fun.

3. AI, VOICE AND CHATBOTS

The use of AI to power the communication and content of loyalty programs is on the increase. AI goes beyond data analytics to look at patterns and predict behaviour – and this is being used by programs to power relevant messaging to the member base. AI is being used to automate customer service (member service) centres, thereby reducing response times and minimising customer/member angst.

Usage of AI powered chatbots is on the rise. Instant response to queries, engagement, product recommendations are all possible through chatbots. Not only is this more efficient, it also reduces costs substantially. Chatbots tend to resolve about 80% of member queries in the first instance.

AI is also being used to harness data for product innovation. In fact, the data generated by loyalty programs can be used to drive decisions across the organisation if used effectively. Remember, your loyalty program most often has your best customers as members. What better way to drive customer wow than use loyalty data to drive enterprise decisions.

Voice assistants like SIRI and ALEXA are being increasingly used to power searches, aid documentation of lists, to-dos etc – and yes, also for shopping. H&Ms voice assistant enables browsing and getting styling advice all through voice prompts.

India is beginning to see the use of chatbots and voice assistants particularly in e-commerce - and also quite frequently in customer/ member service.

A word of caution here. While there is undeniable efficiency being brought to the table by the use of AI, it will do good for loyalty initiatives not to forget the human element. Machine understanding can never replace human empathy completely and this will soon become a point of differentiation for loyalty initiatives as more and more of the processes are automated.

4. OF META AND THINGS NFT

"Starbucks Brewing Revolutionary Web3 Experience for its Starbucks Rewards Members" was a headline in 2022. Starbucks Odyssey - an extension of Starbucks Rewards - allowed members to earn and buy digital collectible stamps (Non-Fungible Tokens or NFTs) that would unlock access to new and immersive coffee experiences. Rewards included virtual classes, curated merchandise or a trip to a Starbucks coffee farm. Buying the NFTs also counted towards elevated tier – and hence elevated proposition.

Starbucks Rewards has been one of the first programs to integrate NFTs into the main program proposition – and at scale. In March 2023, Starbucks launched a paid collection of 2000 NFTs (Digital stamps) each priced at USD 100 – They sold out in under twenty minutes.

Dozens of big brands have been making tentative forays into the NFT world – Taco Bell, Nike, Adidas to name a few. People's willingness to spend on virtual novelty items – such as accessories for an avatar – is a growing trend, and one that bodes particularly well for the future of loyalty marketing, as it lends credence to the immense potential of NFTs. Brands are just beginning to experiment with NFTs in their loyalty initiatives, be it as tokens that unlock VIP perks and deals, or branded digital collectibles that have intrinsic value.

If loyalty is about driving consistency and stickiness, then the concept of collectibles through NFTs should work. Because the collectibles are DIGITAL and not physical, the challenge it to make them unique and desirable. And constantly innovate to keep them desirable!

An oft quoted example is the BORED APE YACHT CLUB – a collection of 10,000 Bored Ape NFTs – unique digital collectibles. Each Bored Ape is a unique digital character generated using more than 170 possible traits, including the ape's clothing, expression, headwear, and more. The NFTs serve as a digital identity which then gets the member access to certain areas of the online Yacht Club and exclusive events. For example, one benefit is that members can access The Bathroom, which is called a "collaborative art experience for the cryptosphere." This means members can paint a pixel on a digital bathroom wall. A more notable benefit is that NFT holders have full commercialization rights to their Bored Apes. If you own a Bored Ape and you want to use it to sell t-shirts, you can.

Branding and partnerships were crucial to the success of the Bored Ape Yacht Club. It caught on with celebrities who then showed off their own collection, increasing the desirability. Since launch in April 2021, the Bored Ape collection shot up in value.

However, NFTs are speculative and, after the initial high levels of enthusiasm, things have considerably cooled down. They are risky. Buying some of the Bored Apes costs as much as a house – and all you get out of it is a digital ape! Most NFTs have little, if any, real world utility – and their sale value depends on their popularity and desirability.

Having a loyalty program rewards catalogue comprising entirely of NFTs does not seem viable. Adding NFTs to the existing redemption options, or earn options - does seem a viable – and, in fact, attractive proposition. It is one way of creating differentiation for the program.

And now, THE METAVERSE that we are hearing so much about. COVID disrupted in-person contact. People turned to virtual meeting spaces and online experiences – even created their own virtual worlds. Advancements in hardware technology encouraged the adoption of augmented and virtual reality thereby lending a starting block for the Metaverse. The actual word "metaverse" was first coined in 1992 by science fiction writer Neal Stevenson, who used the term to refer to the 3D virtual world in his novel Snow Crash. Today, the metaverse is a convergence between real and virtual world experiences. Metaverse is AMBIENT COMPUTING – being IN the computer, versus accessing the computer. It essentially combines the immersive nature of Virtual Reality with the connectivity of Social Media. Bloomberg estimates the Metaverse to become a USD 800 Bn market by 2024 - and evolve into a USD 8 trillion market over the next two decades!

So, what's the relevance for loyalty? Think virtual programs, virtual shopping, virtual events, virtual gamification – and yes, virtual rewards (NFTs). Brands are developing their own Metaverses using gamification and loyalty features. **The combination of the Metaverse and the real world makes for unique loyalty offerings.**

Alibaba and Burberry held a joint initiative, where purchasing a unique NFT in the Metaverse meant that the buyer gets rewarded with an exclusive Burberry scarf only available to people with the NFT.

Snoop Dogg has his very own mansion in the Sandbox Metaverse. Loyal fans who regularly attend his concerts and buy his merchandise can obtain passes to visit the virtual mansion for events, participate in games for rewards and even interact virtually with the rapper.

Marriott combined the Bonvoy program with NFTs and Metaverse. They created **3 different digital art pieces in the form of NFTs**. These NFTs **act as the access passes into Marriott's Metaverse**. Additionally, NFT holders were also able to attend the Art Basel event in Miami for a chance to win 200,000 reward points from Marriot Bonvoy. 3 Lucky winners that held their NFT were chosen. An interesting way to leverage the program, the program currency and keep it desirable.

The concept of the Metaverse and NFTs are both still nascent and all ventures into this world are as yet tentative. After the initial euphoria, there is a more cautious and measured approach to both which ultimately bodes well for a more stable future. Given that the basic principles underlying both are engagement, stickiness and virality, they are a perfect fit for new-age loyalty as long as the fundamental loyalty principles of design are adhered to.

Stick to the basics first – It's not that hard!

IN CONCLUSION

We have travelled the long journey from conception to design to execution of loyalty initiatives. It is a world of opposites that co-exist seamlessly and in marvellous symphony.

Think of it as composing a piece of music with a multi-piece orchestra at play.

Loyalty is a philosophy that must be driven top-down, with intent and commitment for it to deliver long-term value. Execution has to be driven bottom-up from the grass-root level, with every customer-facing employee empowered to drive delight.

Loyalty will have several deliverables. It is accountable and measurable. But there is one single lighthouse metric that must guide all initiatives. And this single metric may change as the program evolves.

Loyalty cannot exist without the hard and tangible benefits. Those are hygiene. Those are the talking points. And loyalty cannot differentiate itself without the soft benefits. Those are what speak the brand's language and express the brand's intent!

Loyalty is about data and what it reveals. But data tells you WHAT has happened. It does not tell you WHY it has happened. Supplement and overlay it with research and customer/member feedback for a holistic view. The importance of spontaneous member feedback cannot be over-emphasised.

Loyalty is empowered by technology. We have seen advancements in leaps and bounds in loyalty hardware, marcom software, AI, voice and chatbots and yes, Metaverse and NFTs. But nothing can replace the human mind to make that leap from insights to brilliance and deliver a value proposition that is truly enticing.

The loyalty program value proposition arises out of a detailed Discovery process that studies the organisation, the environment, the customer and the competition. Once the guardrails are in place, it takes a leap of faith, a leap of intent and a leap of brilliance to create a compelling value proposition and program offering.

Loyalty is all about communicating relevantly. And yet, most communication is digital these days. How do we make an impact in 160 characters or an email headline to drive home this relevance.

Loyalty is accountable and measurable. The hard metrics of enrolment, transaction, repeat and retention are proof of the program's performance. But the true staying power of the program is also measured in the softer metrics of engagement, satisfaction, recommendation and word-of-mouth.

Welcome to this wonderful world of contradictions and collaboration! I hope you enjoyed the journey. This is just the beginning!

Printed in the USA
CPSIA information can be obtained
at www.ICGtesting.com
LVHW050448020324
773349LV00011B/279